From Innocence to Reality

Dear Ann,

One of the greatest blessings Tia and I have received by having our shop is the relationships we have formed with people such as you. We are honored by your friendship, and I am honored you chose to purchase and read my memoir From Innocence to Reality. Thank you.

Patricia Simms Harrison

May 24, 2003

From Innocence to Reality

✦

A Family Memoir

Patricia Simms Harrison

Writers Club Press
New York Lincoln Shanghai

From Innocence to Reality
A Family Memoir

Writers Club Press
an imprint of iUniverse, Inc.

For information address:
iUniverse, Inc.
2021 Pine Lake Road, Suite 100
Lincoln, NE 68512
www.iuniverse.com

ISBN: 0-595-26275-9

Printed in the United States of America

I dedicate this work to my husband Keith and to our children, Tia, Karry, Scott, Sean and Dirk, who have continually given me their support, understanding and love without questions or demands. Because of them, I have possessed the strength to pursue this endeavor without surrendering.

Contents

Part VI

Expression of Gratitude

Did I remember to tell you how grateful I am? I only wish I were capable of adequately expressing my appreciation. If I had not enrolled in Dr. Patrick Grace's Life Writing Class during the early part of 2001, this book would not have been completed. For years, I had saved letters, pictures, newspaper articles, depositions, legal papers, and wills, hoping to recognize when the proper time had arrived for me to attempt writing an account of what I perceived happened when my father and brothers sued my husband Keith for his 40 shares of "The Piece Goods Shop, Inc." Noticing an article in the *Huntington Herald Dispatch* concerning this class, I decided the hour had arrived. Little did I realize what immense blessings God was bringing to me. Yet, being God, he knew how much assistance I was going to need.

Dr. Grace was a mentor who was capable, loving, understanding, patient, but mainly he was motivating. And, as if that was not sufficient, every member of our class displayed the identical attributes. I am truly grateful to all of you.

Another person to whom I am extremely indebted is Dr. Harold T. Murphy. I met him in the fall of 1961, when I decided to return to college to obtain a degree in secondary education. I was thirty-four years old, a wife, and a mother of five; yet, I forged ahead. During this era, older students were discouraged from beginning studies in higher education. I regret having to admit to this; but, after making several appointments with one of the college deans to plan my course of study, I realized I had to resort to more drastic actions. Therefore, during my next appointment, I allowed a few tears to escape from my eyes and roll down my cheeks, resulting in my finally receiving a plan of study and a fall schedule. Thus began my trip into the world of academe.

The first class in which I enrolled was a Spanish class taught by Dr. Murphy. He was the perfect person and teacher for me at that point in my life. Under his tutelage, I discovered I had not completely forgotten what I had learned while attending other schools and colleges. He continued to be important to my completing a bachelor's degree and to achievements in higher fields of learning. When I defended my dissertation for the doctorate, he was present during the actual defense (with a bottle of champagne). After I finished the manuscript for this book, he kindly agreed to proofread it. Since the first day I entered his classroom, he has been a warm and compassionate friend, who has willingly shared his wisdom and humor. Muchas gracias, mi amigo.

Of course, if it had not been for my wonderful and giving daughter Tia, this story would still be in long hand and few would be enticed to read it. However, Tia agreed to become my personal typist. God himself is the only person who knows how many pages she has typed just so I could complete this one work. In addition, she served as an advisor and proofreader, offering advice such as, "Mama, you have already said that," or "That isn't the way I remember it," or "Is that the correct spelling?" Yet, what I appreciated the most of all has been her being there for me, regardless of what was happening in her personal life or what day or hour it was. I am positive she prays I shall not attempt another opus. Well, my darling, not even I know what tomorrow shall bring, but, whatever it is, I shall need you with me. I love you, your Daddy loves you, and so does your creator.

Now, I turn to Keith, my husband, father of our five children, confidante and lover. When I first began researching, organizing and writing this account, Keith read every word, offering his comments; however, after a few chapters, he declared, "This is your book, Patty, and you must make the decisions," and so I have. Yet, he has been an obvious and constant force, especially when I have become too involved with the abstract. As usual, he has struggled to return me to what he believes is reality. So, as a reward, my love, you and I shall share ourselves for another fifty years, for we truly "have found our own."

Not last but always, I give praise and gratitude to my Lord and Savior, who created me and has been with me throughout every living moment of my life. Oh, God, what joy you have given me. I extol your name and give you my love and devotion. May my spirit and words be truthful in your sight, so I shall continue to live with you on earth and in heaven.

From Innocence to Reality begins with a vivid and detailed description of the family's usual activities on Christmas Eve. After celebrating the birth of Christ at their church, the author's husband Keith, their five children and she drive to the home of one of her brothers, Dudley III, who is giving a holiday party. In the midst of the festivity, Dudley appears with several business forms for Keith to sign. However, as there are problems with the electrical system within the house, Keith is unable to decipher what is printed on the paper. At the close of Chapter One, Keith realizes he is being asked to release his forty percent interest in the family business "The Piece Goods Shop, Inc."

A description of the events on Christmas Day 1970 introduces the saga which is developed by the author's describing the relationships between the author and her husband and with their families, relatives and friends. Memories are recounted through personal stories and letters, legal papers, newspaper articles, wills and depositions. Harrison leads us from the innocence of youth through the reality of experience, her purpose being to reveal what happens to the Harrison and Simms families when love for success, money and power gains prominence over God's command to love one another.

PART I

o o o o o o o o o o o o o o o o o o o o o o o o o o o o o o o o

Pity would be no more

If we did not make somebody Poor;

And Mercy no more could be

If all were as happy as we.

—Verse 1
"The Human Abstract
by
William Blake, 1794

1

Christmas Eve 1970

Christmas has always been my favorite time of the year. I believe this is due to the feeling of hope which is so evident from the beginning of Advent until Epiphany Sunday. Of course, there are those who may declare only Christians receive this Christmas blessing of hope, but I disagree. Hope is contagious; it passes from one person to another, begetting love, anticipation and joy. However, it is strange that each year, during this period of time, a complete feeling of hope suddenly appears and ends just as sharply, reminding me of the falling snow in a glass water ball. The snow begins to fall when the ball is shaken and ceases a short time later, giving intermittently a reward from the tribulations of life to those in attendance.

The Christmas season of 1970 began with that usual presence of hope filled with love, anticipation and joy. I was teaching at Huntington High School, and my husband Keith was working in the finance department of the Huntington city government. In addition to our customary responsibilities, we attended programs at church, planned holiday activities for family and friends, decorated our home and prepared gifts. By the arrival of Christmas Eve, we were anxious to commence the celebration of our Savior's birth. Our daughter Tia and her husband Joe were joining us at church. Riding with us in our car were our four sons: Karry, the oldest son, was home for a Christmas break from West Virginia Wesleyan College; next was Scott, who was fifteen and, as usual, anticipating an evening of fun and frolic; Sean, fourteen years old, was on leave from Greenbrier Military School in Lewisburg, and last was Dirk, our youngest son, thirteen years old and content to be with his siblings on this special night.

Driving to church was never a simple act for us. First, it was necessary for all to be ready to depart from home at approximately the same moment, and secondly, the seating arrangement had to be approved by each passenger before our departure. By omitting either or both of these activities the entire evening's festivities might have been destroyed. Yet, leaving the house in one body was relatively easy this night. Keith decided to go directly to the problem and chance gaining a rapid solution by ordering, "Get into the car, sit down in a vacant space and be quiet." It was a miracle; each son followed instructions without debate.

Traditionally, on Christmas Eve, our family sat near the front of the sanctuary, on the left side, resulting in no need for complete searches of the church to find each other before, during and after the service. Another tradition I particularly anticipated was one suggested by the church council itself. All those who were attending the program were asked to enter and leave the sanctuary in silence. This complete absence of voice created a remarkable aura of peace, a priceless gift, especially on December 24. I remember finding our seats in the pew and exhaling a sigh of relaxation. I gazed from one side of the room to the other, hypnotized by the lighted evergreen tree decorated with Christian symbols and by the candles burning in front of each stained glass window, as well as by the ocean of poinsettias announcing the arrival of Christ's day of birth. No matter how often I had seen the church decorated in preparation of this season, it always fascinated and excited me. Finally, the choir and the ministers proceeded down the center aisle to their positions in the choir loft and the pulpit. Following were the appropriate meditation, the communion, and the appearance of church members dressed as the holy family and as angels, shepherds and wise men. Interspersed throughout the hour was the singing of carols, ending with "Joy to the World" and each person holding a lit candle. Though these events were not novel, they continued to be effective and moving. They had never failed to prepare us for the holiday activities, which followed the repasts of worship and praise. Unaware of what was to take place after the Christmas service of 1970, we proceeded with our planned activities. We blew out our candles and departed for the home of my brother Dudley and his family who, at this time, were living on Twelfth Street and Ritter Park.

It was a lovely drive from the church to the house. We purposely passed through the downtown area to view the lights that were hanging on the lampposts and in shop windows. Then, turning south on Eight Street, we continued until we reached Ritter Park. The sight of beautiful homes, dressed in Christmas garb, forming a frame around the edges of the park, aroused feelings of gratitude and happiness within our hearts. We were so blessed to have all of our family together, especially during this season. As our children were growing older and more independent, it was becoming impossible to be together as often as we had been in past days and years. We praised God for affording us the opportunity to regroup and to enjoy each other's love once again.

Keith parked on Twelfth Street, and we actually rushed out of the car, talking and playing as we walked up the drive to the front porch. While knocking on the huge door of the Simms house, I was reminded of the transformation which had occurred within the last year. Barbara, Dudley's wife, and he had bought an old Spanish style pebble-dashed house and changed it into a gorgeous Georgian brick colonial adorned by four Ionic pillars which were standing tall on the front veranda, announcing to all who passed that those who lived within this structure had achieved success, wealth and social status.

Dudley answered the door with the customary greetings of love and welcome. We entered through the front hall and, after removing our outer clothing, turned left into the main living room. The inside of the house was even more impressive than the outside. During the renovation, crown molding had been added around the tops of the walls, silk brocade drapes and valances were hung at the windows, oriental rugs covered the wood floors, cut-velvet chairs and sofas were placed in perfect positions for comfort and appearance, crystal chandeliers dripped from the ceilings, and, as the finishing touch, there appeared a grand piano. The scene was breathtaking to behold. Of course a magnificent Christmas tree was standing in one corner, the perfect companion for a Christmas celebration. In addition, candles, large and small, were evident throughout the house. Then passing through the French doors which led from the living room, one entered the dining room, which had been prepared to satisfy and respond to the desires of those fortunate enough to be present. The piece de resistance was the buffet supper presented on a freshly polished mahogany sideboard located against the wall just opposite the opened doors. The offering included most of the traditional Christmas delicacies: Smithfield ham, sliced paper thin (my favorite), hot biscuits, dips, crackers, salads, casseroles, desserts, coffee, tea and punch (non-alcoholic). The feast was prepared; the stage was set. Little did we suspect that we were the main characters.

Dudley walked with us into the living room, announcing, "John called from Charleston this afternoon. He should be here soon." John and Dudley are my brothers who also happen to be twins. They were born when I was almost ten years old and Betty (our sister) was almost eight. They had always been special people, but their most outstanding attribute was being male. Males were lacking in our family, as Daddy had eight female siblings and Mother had two; neither one had a brother. I vividly remember thinking, on the day they were born, that the entire town of Charleston was celebrating. As I said before, i was not yet ten, so my point of view was limited. In addition to being boys, they were extremely attractive, even as babies. They possessed softy curled hair which was light brown, complimenting their dark brown eyes. Dudley, who was born ten minutes before John, was named after Daddy (Dudley, Jr.) and Daddy's dad (Dudley, Sr.). John was the namesake of Mother's father.

Through the years, they grew more handsome and attracted attention wherever they ventured. Dudley had moved to Huntington in 1961, replacing my husband Keith as manager of The Piece Goods

Shop in Huntington, West Virginia. John was living in Winston-Salem, North Carolina, where he managed another Piece Goods Shop. This year John, his wife Victoria, their daughter and baby son were spending the holidays in Charleston. Expecting to be with them the next day for the family dinner at Mother and Daddy's home, I was actually surprised to hear Dudley say John was driving to Huntington that evening. Being curious, I asked, "Who is coming with him?" I was certain Mother and Daddy would not travel to Huntington on Christmas Eve, and I couldn't believe Victoria and the children would agree to visit Huntington after the trip from Winston to Charleston, especially as the baby was less than six weeks old. Answering my question, Dudley replied, "Oh, he is coming alone. John had a meeting at the lawyers' office this afternoon, and he is bringing some papers that Dad wants me to read before tomorrow." This was an answer but not a satisfactory one, in my estimation; however, as the house was filled with friends and children, I decided not to pursue the topic. I recall thinking, "I will attempt to ask him later. Anyway John will probably tell us the circumstances when he arrives." Naivete has always been a trait of mine, even to this day, and I believe it has often made my life more content. Being suspicious is so time-consuming and mind altering.

After this brief interlude, I decided to find my sister-in-law Barbara. I assumed she would be in the kitchen, and I was correct. She was busily cooking and overseeing other events necessary to pleasing approximately thirty people. Barbara was and is a perfect wife. Dudley and she met at Stonewall Jackson High School while they were students. They had often declared that neither had ever dated anyone else. They married in 1958 and later (1961) moved to an apartment in Huntington, only three blocks from where we lived and continue to live. When their family began growing, they moved to another house which was located on a hill further away from us, and finally to their present location. While I was living at my parents' home, I often cared for John and Dudley; even after I married, I was with them a great deal. Keith was fascinated with my brothers and they with him. They would go camping, play ball together, view basketball and football games, play pool and ping pong, and he even taught them to drive a car. After Dudley and Barbara's move to Huntington, our daughter Tia frequently cared for Troy (their first child) and the other children, as they were born. All of our children were especially close to Troy and lovingly named her Baby Troy. To this day, they speak of Baby Troy who now is married and has two children of her own.

Barbara and Dudley also joined the same church which we had attended since 1949, The Fifth Avenue Baptist Church. They b came valued members and developed close relationships with many who came there to worship and to serve the Lord. It was not unusual for us to visit with them at the church and at our homes. As far back as I am aware, I have thanked God for blessing me with the gift of having Betty, John and Dudley as my siblings. At times they may have performed in certain ways or said something with which I did not agree, but not one of us is perfect. I trust they would say the same about me. I rejoice in believing God's love for us is constant, never changing, no matter what we may say or do, and believe he expects us to love each other as he loves us. I love my brothers and their families and pray they will always love me and those who are mine.

Within an hour after we had arrived at Barbara and Dudley's home, John parked his car in the driveway and knocked at the door. He entered with his usual smiles, hugs and kisses. I was so happy he had decided to come; it had been months since we had been together. After the excitement had subdued, I inquired, "How is the new baby? We all are so anxious to see him. Is his hair really red? I have always wanted a child with red hair. I know he is beautiful."

John then responded, "Victoria and the children wanted to come with me tonight, but there was so much I had to do this afternoon. I decided it was best for me to come alone." At this moment, I noticed that both John and Dudley appeared more nervous and tense than they usually were. Of course, their normal delivery of speech often displayed hesitant and staccato traits. As children, they had developed a pattern of speech which was difficult for others, except for the two of them, to understand. During this period, they had received treatment by a speech therapist. In fact, one of the most memorable days of my life was connected to their going to the therapist. It was October 1, 1947. Keith and I were staying at 401 Fairview Drive, Mother and Daddy's home, due to their being in New York City on a buying trip. I had planned to meet John and Dudley after school and drive them to the therapist's office. After dressing, I began to walk down the steps to the main floor, when I felt a gush of water escape from between my legs. If I had not been forewarned of such an occurrence, I might have become astonished and frightened. However, our first child was due within a week, so I surmised the water was an indication Keith and I were to become parents a few days earlier than expected. My first thought was, "How am I to drive to John and Dudley's school and take them to their appointment?" Keith was working at The Peoples Store, and I didn't want to bother him. I decided to contact my doctor, and he gave me permission to drive them to their session before going to the hospital. Thus, John and Dudley were able to see their therapist, and Keith would return from work in ample time to reach the hospital for the birth of our first child, especially as Tia had not arrived until shortly after midnight on October 2.

When John and Dudley began going to the therapist, the doctor explained they had developed their own method of communication. When it became necessary for them to converse with others, John and Dudley would endeavor to speak so others might understand them. Being aware of this situation allowed me to recognize signs which would not have been understood by someone less knowledgeable of the situation. If John or Dudley was unreasonably nervous or under stress, it often was demonstrated in his speech. I believed this might have been one of those situations for Christmas is also known as a season of stress as well as joy.

Quickly John and Dudley disappeared into another room explaining, "We're sorry to leave you for a few minutes, but Dad wants us to finish this business tonight. We won't be long." About five minutes later, most of the lights flickered and the house became dark, except for the burning of the candles. As the building had been rewired during the renovation, I considered the problem to be connected with the new electrical system. In addition, there were excited children in each room; perhaps one of them wandered to the basement. I turned to Keith, asking, "Where are the boys? Should we look for them?" I knew Joe and Tia were in the living room with Karry, so we headed in that direction. Maybe we could convince Karry to search for Scott, Sean and Dirk. As we entered the living room from the kitchen, John and Dudley appeared from the other side of the house. Dudley had some papers in his hand. Immediately I thought, "They must be the papers John brought with him from Charleston. Now Dudley won't be able to read them, unless someone locates the electrical circuits. Well, it certainly won't be John and Dudley. They are just like Daddy when it comes to repairing problems around a house. About the only thing they are able to do is change a light bulb, and there are times when they aren't able to do that. I imagine Keith will have to find the box, but how will he find it? He doesn't even have a flashlight in the car, and I can't imagine Dudley knowing where one is. All of us will have to leave. Oh, poor Barbara, she will be so disappointed after doing all the work for this party. And, what will they do tonight about Santa coming and then having to prepare for tomorrow?" I had just completed this conversation with myself, when Dudley walked over to Keith with a pen in one hand and the papers in the other. Reaching the area where Keith was standing, he began to explain "Keith, Dad had John bring these papers here tonight. He says you have to sign them now. It can't wait until tomorrow. They must be taken to the lawyers immediately."

Keith looked puzzled, as if he couldn't quite understand what Dudley was saying. Finally, he asked, "What are they, Dudley? I don't know what Dad would want me to sign tonight, do you? It can't be anything concerning the store because I haven't been there for almost ten years. What do you think they are, Dudley?"

Now it was evident that John and Dudley were both excited and anxious. They began talking rapidly, at the same time, in loud sounds. It was difficult to understand the words, much less the sentences. In fact, if they were speaking in sentences, no one was able to discern the meaning of them. Desperately, Dudley pushed the pen and papers into Keith's hands, saying, "I am not certain what they are, just some forms which the lawyers say you must sign. You know how lawyers are constantly wanting papers signed for no reason." Keith was becoming increasingly disturbed. It was evident he did not know what to do. Finally, he explained, "Dudley, I can not do this. I can not sign these papers until I have read them, and there is not enough light." Then, as if he possessed the power to illuminate the room, Keith crossed to a table with a lit candle on it. He lowered the papers toward the candle and squinted his eyes, attempting to decipher the typed message. He raised his head and faced Dudley. Bewildered by what he believed was the message in the documents, he cried, "Dudley, these papers appear to be forms giving my shares in the Huntington Piece Goods Shop to you and John and Dad? Is that what these are, Dudley? They can't be."

Dudley then answered, "Yes, Dad wants you to give the stock back to us. As you said, you haven't had anything to do with the store for almost ten years. Why do you think you should keep the stock? It is not yours, and it is important for you to give it to us now."

Still confused, Keith responded, "What will I receive in return?" Dudley harshly answered, "Just what you gave for them. Nothing. You gave nothing for them, so you receive nothing in return. Why do you think you deserve something?"

"Dudley, you can't believe that I did not earn these stocks. They were promised to me when Patty and I left Illinois and came to West Virginia. I left my birthplace, my parents, my brother, my grandparents, friends I grew up with, my church. Patty and I were even planning to build a house on the lot my parents gave us when we were married. And, what about the years I worked in the store from 1949 to

1961? Even Patty worked there when she was able. The store did not operate alone, by itself. You know what a business requires."

It appeared strange that John did not comment; at this point, I can't recall his even being there. I have considered his having returned to Charleston after being assured Dudley had the papers and understood what was needed. Dudley usually accepted the lead position, and it was possible they had decided that, if Keith did not agree to sign the papers at once, he might consider releasing the stocks if there were only one of them. The two of them could be overwhelming, as well as confusing to those around them, and Keith did not respond well to others demanding him to behave according to their wishes and not his own. John and Dudley were acquainted with Keith's mentality and character; for this reason, it appeared odd they assumed Keith would sign any piece of paper before his reading it. If Keith is not certain of the situation, he chooses the defensive position and remains with it until he is proven incorrect, and the more the opposite side argues, the more he solidifies his stance.

After Keith's convincing Dudley he was not signing the papers, at least until he had completely read them, Keith offered to examine the electrical system. I can't explain his decision, but he did find the problem and solved it at once. He claims to remember that the breaker he switched on was #13. Of course, following the confrontation, the previous mood of the evening changed to dejection and perplexity. It was as if the glare of the now functioning lights revealed what before had been hidden. We decided it was time to gather our clan and return to our house at "1016."

Nevertheless, Christmas Eve 1970 had not yet reached its end; several hours remained. Most people would have expected us to return home midst shouts of anger and recriminations, but that was not us. We attempted to recapture feelings of hope by praying that what we had just experienced would perish with the close of the eve, never to return. Keith and I then began our customary pilgrimage throughout the neighborhood, ending at our house with champagne and hors d'oeuvres. By the time we had finished our neighborhood gathering, Christmas morn had arrived and our children were asleep. To this day, the event does not appear real. True, I have attempted to describe the happenings of Christmas Eve 1970; however, it is as if I were writing about what happened to others, not to us. How could our family have been trapped in such a shocking drama? Perhaps we misunderstood the actions and the intentions of those involved. But, living through the last thirty years has finally convinced me to accept the reality of the events which occurred on Christmas Eve 1970 and afterwards.

Now, I find myself questioning the reason for my refusing to acknowledge what truly happened. Perhaps it was due to faulty thinking. I believed each family member would forever continue the love and faith for each other, which had been woven into our souls; that nothing would destroy this relationship. This premise was supported by a letter, which Mother wrote to me on Tuesday, October 23, 1945. At this time, I was studying at Ward-Belmont in Nashville, Tennessee. Mother had just returned to Charleston after having visited with me for three days. In the last paragraph, she discusses our family.

When you write your daddy and me be sure to thank him for mailing the cake and the chewing gum. He wanted and did help to lift the cake into the box. He wanted to know all about everything and I know he was sorry he couldn't go with me to see you, so be sure to especially mention his coming on Thanksgiving. He was quite proud of your grades. God has been so good to me and my family. If he only stays with me to see my family to the same happiness that he has given me—lovely, healthy, sweet, and good daughters and sweet sons. Yes, they are sweet and thoughtful at times, and the best of husbands, even if he has a strong voice (smile). You know, Patty, there really aren't many families like we are. We aren't fancy, but I like the way we all are and I want our children to find in their mates those things that they are used to. Mrs. Burgess just called from the Diamond and is sending you six pairs of cotton knit panties and please take care of them. They are so hard to find.

All my love,

Mother

The following day I wrote Daddy a note thanking him for caring for Dudley and John so Mother would be able to visit me in Nashville. However, I also made him aware that I wished everyone could have come with her. I ended by saying even though I was tired, I was preparing my Spanish assignment. I am certain I did just that.

On the evening Mother left Nashville, Sunday, October 21, 1945, I wrote:

Dear Mother,

It was so wonderful having you here this weekend. I really know I could not have waited until Thanksgiving to see you all. Until I left home and missed everyone so, I never knew how much we meant to each other. I can hardly wait for all of the Simms family to be here. Everyone says they have to meet the rest, after meeting you. I certainly thank Betty Lee and Daddy for letting you come.

This afternoon Beverly and I just fooled around in our room. I tried to study chemistry; I ended by writing letters. It was dreary this afternoon. It rained while we were in dinner.

Thank you for being you.

Love,

Patty

2

Pleas and Demands

The day following the episode at Dudley's was Christmas Day 1970. I could not conceive of any way, possible or impossible, to avoid its dawning, except perhaps a complete destruction of the universe, but God must not have seen that as a justifiable solution. As Tia was now married, her husband and she were celebrating Christmas morning with his family. We had made arrangements to meet them at Mother and Daddy's later that afternoon. Our sons had reached the stage where sleep was more desirable than gifts, so we remained in bed until about nine-thirty. We shot the usual movies of the boys descending the steps, but they were not as detailed or lively as those taken in previous years, especially those which recorded what happened following Santa's Christmas visit. After the boys had lumbered down the steps, I said to them, "Please try to forget last night, at least until this afternoon. We must not allow what happened to ruin the entire celebration."

Traditionally, we exchanged gifts before eating breakfast, so we followed our previous plans. Scott, Sean and Dirk each received sound and record equipment, and we gave Karry a piece of luggage. Keith surprised me with a one hundred dollar bill, folded minutely and placed in a small ring box. I presented him with the customary blazer, shirt and tie. There were articles of clothing for everyone except Karry. No one who knew Karry would have had the courage to present him with clothing, unless Karry had personally selected it. Even then, the giver was taking a chance of something being wrong, and, if this happened, Karry's insisting that what he had received was the perfect gift. He would enthusiastically say, "This is the very sweater I wanted. I didn't really think anyone would know what I needed at school to keep me warm." Then, years later, I would find several gifts from past Christmases (including the sweater) stored in a trunk which was kept in his closet. To say Karry was difficult to please is being kind. This is a fact, not a criticism; Karry's taste has always been above reproach. He definitely has a flair for assembling a wardrobe which few other males possess.

After the opening of gifts, Keith and I prepared our customary Christmas breakfast of ham, eggs and biscuits. While we were occupied in the kitchen, our sons entertained friends who had stopped by to talk and plan activities during their vacations. Keith actually cooked the food; I set the table. This meant that anyone who expected to eat had to run to the table immediately when Keith announced, "Breakfast is ready. Come now." Arriving at the table, we joined hands, thanked our Lord for our blessings, and ate our meal, as if this Christmas were the same as all others had been. The last duty, before departing for Charleston, was to dress. Going to Mother and Daddy's for a holiday dinner demanded a more formal attire than if we had remained at home. This was not something we resented, at least it wasn't for me. I enjoyed seeing the males in suits and the females in party frocks. We were having a celebration in honor of Christ's birth, and I was proud to declare we were dressed for the occasion. For years, I had assumed our family enjoyed Christmas evening in Charleston as much as I did, for I had never heard any complaints, though new toys and gifts were left behind in Huntington. The children were aware they would find more presents at "401" and they would be able to socialize with their cousins.

Getting into the car on Christmas Day was not the problem we faced on the previous night. The rowdy and noisy group had become solemn and silent. What was there to say or do? We could not be certain of what lay ahead of us, when reaching our destination. Mentally I questioned our being permitted to enter; however, remaining in Huntington might have been equated to our surrendering to their demands. Therefore, we silently entered the car and closed the doors. I felt as if we were about to visit the world of the unknown.

The weather even complimented our dark and somber moods. Traveling fifty miles on the highway provided time and space for my thoughts to wander. I gazed through the windows at sights I had seen countless times before. However, this afternoon, instead of the sights serving as distractions, they became a setting conducive to creating mental images, enticing me to a hypothetical world of supposition.

I was reminded of an old hymn written by Henry Hyde during the nineteenth century, titled "What We Are Is What We Become." In it, he offered that what we choose is what we are and what we love is what we shall be. The goal may ever be in the distance, but, by God's giving us the right to choose, he has made us free, free to choose to be right or wrong, to be good or evil. I thought I had chosen to be good; however, beyond this decision, I faced constant situations which forced me to choose again. Though I prayed to God to show me the way, to reveal his will to me, often the results proved I had chosen my will, not God's. Miraculously, God would forgive me, and I would again endeavor to please him.

At first, I would act as if the mistake had been erased and my record was as free of sin as it had been in the beginning. Yet, we all realize this is not what occurs. Actions have results, results which affect other lives, environments, countries, thoughts, behaviors. The effects are limitless. According to natural law, actions can not be erased nor can time be reversed. While driving to Charleston on Christmas Day 1970, I questioned in my mind whether the decision to return to West Virginia was made according to my will or God's. We could just as easily have shown our gratitude to Mother and Daddy for offering us such a wonderful opportunity and then explained that we felt morally obligated to remain in Illinois. Imagine how different all of our lives would have been. Yet this was not the path we chose. I remember being gloriously happy to return to West Virginia and to my family. Though Keith and I discussed the decision and though he declared it was as much his decision as mine, I know he consented to leave Illinois because of his love for me and the promise of a more comfortable life for our family than the one in Freeport. Now, if I had demanded we leave, his answer would have been, "Definitely not. My mother and dad have been expecting me to work in the grocery business, and I cannot disappoint them. We talked about this over and over again and you knew where we were going to live." Keith does not respond kindly to a person dictating what he is to do or say.

Our arrival in Charleston ended my period of mental discussion. We had reached Mother and Daddy's house, so slowly we removed ourselves from the car. Also, we had presents to gather, carry in and place under the tree. This year Mother had used Della Robbia garland and lights around the front door. Angels were hung on each side of the entrance, heralding the birth of the Christ child. The door was unlocked, leaving us free to enter without knocking. Most of the adults were in the living room. We attempted the usual holiday salutations, but hearing the words as they escaped from our lips, we realized they were false. How could anyone experience a "Merry Christmas" on a day such as this?

My memories of that day, including the rest of the holiday, are fragmented and often vague, due to the passing of time and the emotions involved. Mother's favorite pastime was decorating, and, as expected during the Christmas holidays, she exceeded all her other presentations. The main tree was delivered ten days before Christmas. For years the tree had been place in the living room, but, this year, it was located in the sun room (which at one time had been a balcony). Enclosing this porch greatly increased the amount of available space. As the sun room opened from the end of the living room, the view of the tree was seen by those occupying the main room or the sun room. The tree was the usual balsam fir, decorated with ornaments Mother had purchased abroad and in the States through the years. As Daddy had functioned in almost every office of the Lion's Club, local and international, they had traveled around the world several times. Underneath the tree was a figure of Santa, kneeling beside the baby Jesus in the manger. Few gifts were placed under this tree because there was not enough space; thus, another tree had been erected in the basement recreation room. It was there we placed our gifts and returned upstairs.

Evergreen wreaths with enormous bows were hung on the inside and outside of each window. Poinsettias, candles, Christmas figures and books were seen and music heard throughout. The help Mother had hired for Christmas had finished setting the tables in the living room, the dining room and the kitchen. The youngest ate at the table in the kitchen, the oldest ones were seated in the dining room and the young adults were in the living room. Finally, it was announced that Christmas dinner was ready to be served. Mother, who adored beautiful clothes, was wearing a pale pink chiffon dress with rhinestones embroidered on the bodice. As she walked toward me, I thought how lovely she looked and silently questioned what she was going to say to me. Placing her arm around my shoulders, she said, "Lets go into the dining room. This may be our last meal together." It was not our last meal forever, but it was the last meal for several years.

The Christmas menu was ham, turkey, mashed potatoes, gravy, sage dressing, sweet potatoes, fresh green beans cooked with bacon for at least three hours, cranberry salad, and freshly baked yeast rolls; for dessert, there were pumpkin, pecan, and mincemeat pies. The menu may have been typical, but the preparation and presentation were not. The tables were set with linen cloths and napkins, bone china, crystal goblets and sterling sliver eating utensils. In the center of the table stood a tall cherub with silk tulle draped around the base. The help served the food and replenished the dishes as needed. When everyone had finished the basic meal, the dinner plates were replaced with dessert and coffee. At the completion of the last course, we left the table and followed the others downstairs for "gift-opening" time. And, while we were exchanging gifts, the help washed the dishes, silver, pots, pans and whatever else had been used during the preparation and eating of the meal. After all articles had been placed where they belonged, the help left to celebrate their own Christmases. Most of the staff who worked during the holidays were very familiar to us. Our lives intertwined. We appreciated the love and care they gave to us, and they appreciated being able to provide for their families with the funds they received from Mother and Daddy. They definitely enriched our lives, and I believe we enriched theirs.

Describing the Christmas of 1970 evokes memories of other Christmases. Christmas 1944 was a very special one for me. Keith was training at the Great Lakes Naval Center near Chicago, Illinois. We had met during the previous September, and we had promised to write to each other every day. It may appear silly to some, but I claim the written expression of ideas and sentiments has made our married life stronger and richer. As soon as Keith finished boot training, he received a leave, so his family and he traveled to Charleston, but not in time for Christmas. I knew Christmas would be entirely different from all the others he had experienced. On the night of Monday, December 25, 1944, I wrote:

Dearest One,

I hope Santa Claus was as nice to you as he was to me. Today has been wonderful. John and Dudley didn't even wake up until nine, thirty. This truly surprised all of us. Then Daddy took movies of us coming down the steps and handing out gifts.

Right now we are at Aunt Jackie's and Uncle Kenneth's. They received some records from the musical "Oklahoma" and they are playing them. Also, everyone is trying to talk above everyone else; John, Dudley, and little Kenny (Aunt Jackie and Uncle Kenneth's son) keep running and shooting in every direction with their new guns and I am trying to write you a letter for I know it will be three in the morning before we arrive home.

All of the family came to our house at five for dinner. After eating, we sat around and talked. About ten o'clock we drove over to Grandmother's. Now it is one o'clock and we have one more place to go. This is a family tradition that I look forward to from one Christmas to the next.

Darling, you would have wondered about my becoming your wife, if you could have seen my presents. Santa brought me one huge doll, a small dog and a little doll. There were comments about my being in my second childhood, but I have always received a doll for Christmas and I hope I always do. I also received a leather notebook and a pen and pencil set with my name on them, a black slip, a darling pair of house slippers with gold sequin trim (from Grandmother), a manicuring set, a bracelet, sachet hangers, hose, boxes, sheet music, earrings and, of course, the grand piano.

(Time passes.)

We just arrived at Aunt Tootsie's and Uncle Jimmy's. Bonnie Lee, their daughter who is three, received a new baby doll and she called it Patty. Her grandmother made three hats for it and some adorable baby dresses. Tootsie painted a doll bed she had white, and painted "Humpty Dumpty" on it.

Keith, they have the sweetest houses. Both Aunt Jackie and Uncle Kenneth and Aunt Tootsie and Uncle Jimmy built their houses the same year as we did, 1941. Aunt Tootsie has antique furniture in her living room the same as we do. When you come home we'll have to visit all of them; that is if you want.

Darling, I want to tell you again how much I love the compact you sent me. It is so pretty, and I just told Betty Lee the other night that one gift I truly wanted this Christmas was a compact. But I really wasn't expecting one, especially one so beautiful.

Did you all have Christmas dinner at the Lakes? I hope so. It would be terrible to be away from home this time of the year and not even receive a holiday meal.

Tootsie gave me a recipe for candy tonight. She made some for Granddaddy and it is delicious, but it does have peanut butter in it.

Keith, I haven't told you what Daddy gave to Mother. Remember, I told you Daddy was keeping it a secret. Well, when he was in New York the last time, he bought a watch with six diamonds around it. It is a Swiss watch. On the card he wrote "We hope you look at this once in a while—The Family." You know how Mother is always late. He also gave her a pair of diamond earrings. When she opened them, she was standing, so she said, "Let me sit down." She was so surprised.

Did your Mother and Dad say they received my card? I hope they did, even if I did put the wrong name on it.

Well, dearest, we all are going to have a two o'clock snack and go home. I am just about asleep. I now know how you feel having to get up while it is still night.

I'll always be yours,

Patty

A few days later, I received the letter Keith had written to me on Christmas Day 1944. He started:

My only,

The first thing I did this morning was open my presents from you. Really, dearest, they were swell and I thank you from the bottom of my heart. The gloves are so nice and they are just what I needed. When we came here, they issued a pair of wool ones to each man but they are not very warm. The fingers are all worn out, so I was wishing for a new pair. The leather writing folder was what I liked best, darling. It is a job trying to keep the stationery from getting wrinkled. I must shove it in and out of my sea bag every time I want to write. It seems that you knew just the right things to send, my sweet. I really do appreciate them, darling. Thank you so much.

Last night I stood watch from twelve midnight until four in the morning. I was thinking of you those first four hours of Christmas, darling. I thought I might even see Santa Claus himself, but I guess I was either too early or too late.

I suppose you will have one swell time at the Christmas dance, love. Be sure to write and tell me how <u>he</u> was and what happened. It is strange asking you how you enjoyed going out with another boy, but I know you were happy and that is what I want most.

As it is Christmas, there were no classes, so we just stayed around the barracks and rested. It seems funny, but all of us enjoyed it.

Must get dressed for church now.

Love that I have never known before

Keith

As I commented earlier, I am unable to recall much of what happened at Mother and Daddy's during the evening of Christmas 1970. Of course, none of us took movies or photos. Tia and Joe said that after dinner, they remained in the recreation room. They explained that they felt as if they were ghosts moving through the house, invisible to the remaining family members and guests. I recently asked Karry what he remembered, and he repeated what Tia and Joe had said. He replied, "Since 1961, when we no longer had the shop, it was as if no one knew we were there, or even cared. I felt as if they tolerated us." Then I asked, "Why didn't you say something to me?" And he answered, "Mama, I knew how much you loved your family and enjoyed being with them. I thought we could endure the situation for a few hours, especially as it made you so happy." How mistaken I had been! I had prided myself on being empathetic, caring and understanding, but my husband and children were the sensitive ones.

What is vivid in my mind are the months that followed. Dudley came to our home and attempted to persuade Keith to release the stock. He declared, "Keith, this is not what we planned. We believed you knew the stock was not yours and you would just sign the papers. We never thought you would refuse to give the stock back to us, as you had not paid for it and as Dad said he had not given it to you."

Then Keith retorted, "What do you mean by saying that Dad didn't give me this stock? There was no reason for us to come here, if we didn't own part of the shop. Why would we move to Huntington unless we were given an interest in the business?"

"We must have all of the stocks, Keith. What do you want in exchange for them?"

Then Keith, attempting to explain to Dudley, replied to him, "As we were leaving the shop in 1961, Patty asked me if we still had the stocks. I told her that we did, but they probably wouldn't be worth much, if they were worth anything at all. We discussed it and decided we wanted the stocks to go to our children when we died. Their worth is not as important as what they depict. They symbolize twelve years of our lives, twelve years of hope and dreams. I realize I wasn't the best manager, but I wasn't the worse either. However, that is not the issue now. The stocks were given to me. I don't care what they are worth. I don't want any money. I believe you are able to devalue them over the years, until they are worth nothing. Why don't you do that? Then everyone will be satisfied. Please let this sleeping dog lie."

Dudley had tears in his eyes. All of us were extremely distraught. During the time Dudley had lived in Huntington, our families had developed a close and loving relationship, at least I believed we had. We embraced and kissed and Dudley left. Yet, this was not the end of the struggle. There were also phone calls; the one I particularly remember was when my sister, Betty Lee, called me at our house and asked me to go to a phone booth and call Mother and Daddy. Thus, I drove to a drive-in restaurant which was about five blocks from our house and called 21-779, a phone number I shall never forget. Several people spoke to me during the conversation. They explained that they believed Keith was listening to the calls at our home and was influencing what I said and did. I tried to convince them that Keith had to work and was not always at home. Also, I reminded them the stocks were not in my name, that they were given to Keith. During the conversation, Mother said, "Patty, you know you are killing your dad. He cannot believe you are doing this to the family. All of us are afraid he will have a heart attack. You will hate yourself when you watch your Daddy's casket being lowered into the ground. Then you will finally realize what you have caused." (Daddy had been stricken with rheumatoid arthritis and tongue cancer.) With desperation, Mother continued, "What is wrong with you, Patty? How can you treat us like this, especially after all we have done for you and the children? There must be another reason for your acting this way. Is Keith threatening you? Don't listen to him. You know we will take care of you and the children. In fact, come home now. Tell him if he does not return the stocks, you will divorce him." With disbelief, I answered, "How can you ask me to say that to Keith? This has nothing to do our marriage. It has nothing to do with my love for you or him. I couldn't possibly ask Keith for a divorce. Besides, even if I were to speak the words, he knows me well enough to realize I would never leave him." As I made this last statement, I felt as if a voice whispered to me, you have spoken to your parents, your sister, and your brothers for the last time. As I returned the receiver to the hook, I heard their sobs, as well as my own.

Later, one day in January 1971, a friend called to say there was an article in the paper declaring Daddy, John and Dudley were suing Keith for the Piece Goods Shop stock. I heard the words, but they had no meaning. Daddy and my brothers would not choose this path; the article was misconstrued. All these thoughts and more came to mind; however, Keith and I were forced into accepting the veracity of the newspaper article when, a few days later, a deputy sheriff delivered a summons to our front door and presented it to our youngest son, Dirk. At the time he was thirteen years of age. Thus, the love I had expected to lead to happiness had become a snare, enticing us to peace, a peace created by fear and greed

PART II

o o o o o o o o o o o o o o o o o o o o o o o o o o o o o o o o o
And mutual fear brings peace
Till the selfish loves increase
Then cruelty knits a snare,
And spreads his baits with care.

—Verse 2
"The Human Abstract"
by
William Blake, 1794

3

Beginnings

Since the winter of 1971, when my father and my brothers sued Keith, resulting in their paying him $91,839.60 for his stock, I have attempted to discover what would end the lasting conflict between the Harrison family and the Simms family. I have assumed, as do most Americans, that all problems have a solution, that the Harrisons and the Simmses would once again become one happy family. Yet, more than thirty years later, the solution has not been revealed. Therefore, as I am now nearing the last stage of my life, I have decided to adopt a different attitude. I shall settle for an examination of the past in order to determine the causes and to banish from my mind the achievement of a reunion between our families. Soon most of us who have been involved in the conflict will be with God in heaven, and those left on earth will neither know nor care. Thus, with the writing of this book, I shall hopefully gain peace, contentment, and acceptance for life as it exists, rather than life as it was before the suit.

This examination has resulted in an exploration of events which have occurred in my life and Keith's, before and after our marriage in 1946. Keith was born and raised in Freeport, a small town in northwestern Illinois. Both he and his father had expected Keith to enter the family grocery business, after his finishing his education. As a teenager, Keith traveled to produce farms and the Chicago market, buying fresh fruit and vegetables for the two stores owned by his family, The Trading Post and The Stop and Shop. Yet, World War II delayed these plans, as it did the plans of many young American men during this time.

In September 1944, Keith decided to join the Navy but was not ordered to report to the Naval Training Center at the Great Lakes until November 16 of that year. Having a few weeks with nothing special to do, Keith decided to visit his Uncle Bob, Aunt Clara, and cousin Bobbi, who were living in Charleston, West Virginia, and were friends of my family. During this visit, Keith and I fell in love. From the night we were introduced, he talked about the family stores and his buying peaches from farmers in southern Illinois and selling them from the back of one of the stores' trucks to wives and mothers in northern Illinois who were anxious to buy fresh fruit. Due to the war, much of the fresh produce was reserved for the Armed Forces, causing a scarcity at the home front. Keith also spoke of his intentions after the conclusion of the war, intimating he would return to Freeport and Harrison's Finer Foods (the name of the company).

By the time Keith left Charleston, a "first date" kiss had grown into plans for a life together. He quickly became acquainted with me and my family, as what free time I had was spent together with him. At this point of my life, I was a senior at Stonewall Jackson High School and was involved with my classes and activities there. Outside of school, I studied voice, piano, and Spanish III. Also, I taught a primary Sunday school class and was an active member of the Baptist Youth Fellowship, and, when I had nothing else to do, I helped at The Piece Goods Shop and cared for my brothers. In addition, I had a social life. Keith often accompanied me as I attempted to fulfill my obligations. My schedule did not seem to dissuade him, and his company added pleasure to my activities.

Keith would be waiting for me by the front entrance when the last school bell of the day rang. I became the envy of all my girl friends for Keith was not only handsome; he was also an available male, a species which was diminishing in number as many of the male students had joined one of the services. Keith was six feet tall, had lovely blue eyes, dark blonde hair and a mid-west accent which created attention immediately. Nevertheless, some of my closest friends asked, "How can you trust a man with that accent?" Although I answered, "The accent doesn't make the man," I considered his speech one of his assets. I soon discovered Keith possessed other assets; he was a person to be trusted, a man on whom I could depend to say what he meant and to mean what he said.

Returning to Freeport, Keith mailed me pictures of himself, his home, his parents, his brother, and even his grandparents. He often wrote about his friends and what they thought of his new love interest. Of course, in all of his letters he described his feelings for me.

Hi Lovely,

This is the third letter I have written you today. Tell me Patty, if I write too much. Is it a bother to receive three letters in one day? I suppose your mother and dad think it is strange that I am writing so often. If that is the case, tell them I am in love with their oldest daughter.

I am very sorry that I can't write any better. I don't know why, but it is difficult for me to put my feelings into words.

Does your mother read my letters? If she does, she probably realizes that I am serious about us. I told Grandmother Harrison about us tonight, so now nearly the entire family knows you. I wish your picture would arrive, so I could show them how lucky I really am.

You know, honey, when I am writing letters to you, you seem so close to me. It is uncanny, but I feel as if you are in the next room instead of seven hundred and fifty miles away.

I hope I receive mail from you Monday because, for a few months, that is the only way we can be in contact with each other. You may think I do write too often, but I will never tire hearing from you.

All the love in the world,

Keith

Keith's letters were the first sincere love letters I had ever received. Other boys had written me letters containing remarks about love, and I would answer their declarations in the same manner. It was a game we played; we wrote the words as a form of entertainment. Keith's letters were different; they radiated with honesty and love. However, I didn't react this way, when we started dating. On our second date, he asked me to marry him. That night I felt certain it was his method of flirting, but, a few weeks later, I was convinced he was describing his true feelings of love, and I responded with the same emotions.

Passing his physical, Keith reported to the Great Lakes for training on Wednesday, November 23, 1944, the day before Thanksgiving. I couldn't believe he was not allowed to remain at home for the holiday, but I soon discovered wars do not wait for anybody or anything. We continued to write to each other almost every day or night. At the beginning of his training, Keith was pleased with being in the service. On November 25, he wrote, "The Navy is a great life, and, no matter how much you read or hear about it, you have no idea what it really is like." By December 10, he was changing his opinion. His company was sent into Chicago to help the postal system. That night he wrote, "We actually slaved last night. We worked in the freight house from nine-thirty in the evening until six in the morning. It was so cold, and, of course, we had to work outside. We must have sorted a million packages, and many of them were bound for Charleston. The job I had was on the dock by the train tracks. I put the packages into certain carts, sorting them by states. I thought of you while I was working."

Nearing the day of his graduation, he was disillusioned, homesick and anxious to know what his next assignment would be. In addition, there had been epidemics of colds, measles, and scarlet fever; bandages on both hands due to blisters; outside temperatures of less than zero degrees, plus final exams. However, by Tuesday, January 30, Keith's spirits were improving. He was going home on Saturday and traveling by train to Charleston on Monday with his parents. They were anxious to meet me and my family. Just before his leave began, he wrote a letter which truly reflects the thoughts and attitudes of most service men during that era.

Dream,

How hectic good old "53" [company 12153] was today with graduation, our last hair cuts, and our pay checks. By Friday night this bunch of sailors will be a bit happier than they were last Christmas eve.

You are always in my thoughts, my darling, and I love you so much. I have never told you this, but, before I met you, I didn't care when the war would end. Naturally, I wanted it to end so lives could be saved, but, for my sake, it didn't seem important. Now the sooner it ends, the better. Then we will be able to marry, and our dreams will come true. Until then we must make do with our "D" day. Monday evening will be here soon and then....

There is so much sickness in our camp, darling, and it is terrible. It seems as if it has come all at one time. One more boy from our company was taken to the hospital today. He has pneumonia, which is bad, but not as bad as the scarlet fever so many have contacted. I will be sad to say good-bye to all of my buddies here. Living with them for nearly three months has helped me to become friends with many of them. As you know, almost all of us are going to sea, so I doubt I will ever see any of them again. I have often wondered how many will be alive when this is over. What we all would like to do is get together after the war and swap tales. Right here in this company we have men who will make this world a better place for our children. I have never stopped to think of it before, but there could easily be some true American heroes here. Everyone back home is worrying about whether we will have to go to sea and fight or not. They also are worrying if we will be wounded or hurt. Believe me, dearest, when I tell you that is the least of our worries. It seems strange that the ones we love are worrying about us here and we are worrying about the ones we love back home.

Darling, after this leave, it may be a year or more until we will be together once again. I want you to realize that, dearest. Do you think your mother would consent to our becoming engaged then, if we still feel as we do now about one and another?

I think, before catching the train Monday, I will buy all the magazines I can find. It will be a long train ride to Charleston and I will need something to do besides sleeping. I know the last two or three hours of travel will be the most tiresome. At 10:05 I will get off the train; one second later you will be in my arms, and I will be the happiest sailor in the world.

I will always love you.
Forever,

Keith

In the letter written the next day, Keith proudly declared that he had graduated ten minutes before. He also said that he and his family would be arriving in Charleston within four days. He left the Lakes on February 3, traveled to Freeport, visited two days, and caught the train to Charleston on Monday morning, February 5. Keith and his parents stepped down off a train car of the Chesapeake and Ohio Railroad at 10:27 P.M., slightly after the scheduled time. They stayed with his Uncle Bob and Aunt Clara. Actually though, they were coming to Charleston to meet me and my family. We had an unbelievable week with each other and our families, which is obvious in the letters we wrote to each other after he returned to Illinois.

February 11, 1945
Sunday

Dear One,

You have been gone exactly three hours, and it seems more like three days. This morning I tried to teach a Sunday school class, but all I could think of was you, so nothing much was accomplished.

Heaven knows when you will receive this letter for I don't know where to send it. I hope you will find out soon what your new address is.

Keith, I will never forget these five days. They have been the five most wonderful days of my life. No one could have asked for a more glorious time. I only wish it could have lasted forever.

I'm sitting in Mother's room at her desk. Betty Lee is reading, and John and Dudley are playing. Mother just went to Grandmother's to have a cup of coffee. Daddy has gone to the store. We are suppose to be cleaning the downstairs but that will come later. Betty and I are going to club meeting after a while. I can't even think about going back to the same old rut. It will seem like a horrible nightmare after a beautiful dream.

I talked to Grandmother this morning. She called to talk about you. All of the family thinks you are wonderful. She said she had never seen a better boy and that Charleston hadn't either. She approves of your choosing a ring. Oh, Keith, I am so happy. What did your parents say? Did you ask them?

Your Aunt Clara was talking to Mother about all of us going with them and your parents and brother to a lake in Wisconsin for a month this summer. Isn't that a great idea?

Keith, don't forget what I told you. If you ever change your mind, don't be afraid to tell me. We'd both want it that way.

(Time passes.)

You've been gone a little over twelve hours now. By this time, you must be in Chicago. How I wish I were with you.

This afternoon Mary Gail, Betty and I went to the movies. We saw "The Princess and the Pirate" and was it lousy. Then we had dinner at the Daniel Boone Coffee Shop and came home. Mother and Daddy have gone to play bridge. Betty and I finished putting John and Dudley to bed, and I am about ready to spank them for the second time.

How was the trip? I thought about you all day. I imagine it was long and tiresome. I get so bored on trains. Did your Mother and Dad stay in Chicago?

I wonder how long it will be before a letter comes from you. I can hardly wait.

Mother, Daddy and Betty have been asking and asking what you said to me while you were here. Daddy really hasn't asked me, but I can tell he wants to ask. I always answer, "Oh, you know, the same old lines." They know we love each other too much to say.

Darling, I was the girl who was going to bed at six. It is after ten now, so I will close.

I love you more than I ever thought I could love anyone.

Forever yours,

Patty

Keith's next letter to me was dated February 12, 1945.

My Dearest Darling,

You know something? You don't. Then I guess I will have to tell you. When a boy loves a girl as much as I love you, it's wonderful. I love you so much, my darling, and I have missed you so much since we left. When you ask me if I love you and if I ever do stop, to tell you, you are wasting your breath. It just goes in one ear and out the other.

We had a long talk on the way back, darling, about our being married. Mom and Dad like you so much, and they think their son could not have found a nicer girl. They also want us to wait until after the war before we marry. However, they gave their consent for us to be engaged, just as soon as I am able to buy the ring.

I am sorry I am not able to give you any news on when my next furlough will be. If it is at all possible, we will be together when it comes. I certainly hope so, for I have been gone from you two days and already I am planning on how and when we will be together again.

You will be going away to school soon, Patty, and there you will meet many fine young men who are not only nice but very good-looking too. Just remember that little Keith is thinking of you always and is so much in love with you that it hurts to be apart from you.

Must close for now, my darling. Love me forever.

Our love will last forever.

Keith

On February 14, the Navy announced Keith had been chosen to remain at the Great Lakes to receive training for becoming a signal-man. The length of the training had not been determined, but he thought it would last until the middle of June 1945. His not being shipped to the west coast right away was a blessed surprise; plus, he was given week-end passes, so he was able to go home as Freeport was only about one hundred miles from the United States Naval Training Center.

Keith wrote Mother on the same day he had written me, February 12, 1945 (the day after he and his parents had left Charleston to return to Freeport).

Dear Mrs. Simms,

Here I am once again at Great Lakes. It is so different from "boot training" that I feel a little lost. They are not as strict with us, and the chow is so much better than it was at Camp Muffet.

Just as in September, you made my visit to Charleston a complete success. I want to thank you for everything and to tell you that I truly appreciate it. I know it was difficult for you with the boys and all.

Mom, Dad, Jack, and I talked of you all during most of the trip back to Illinois. I am sure that Mom and Dad both think the Simms family is about the best one alive.

Mom and Dad realize now that the love Patty and I have for one another is real and will last forever. Mother thinks Patty is so sweet, and Dad told me that she was far superior to any other girl that I have ever known.

Thank you again for everything, and I hope to be seeing you before long.

As ever,

Keith

Then on March 5, 1945, Keith again wrote Mother.

Dear Mrs. Simms,

This morning your much-welcomed letter came. I understand perfectly how hard it is for you to find time to write, especially with the work you have at home and the store. I think the reason it took so long for the letter to reach me was it was addressed to my old address.

You know, Mrs. Simms, I can see you playing the piano. The next time I see you, you will be a wizard at it. It helps to have daughters that know how to play as well as Patty and Betty do.

The comic strip of Blondie and her troubles putting her children to bed that you sent with the letter certainly reminded me of you and the boys. John and Dudley are the best in my estimation, and if they were little angels, you wouldn't know what to do. If you think they misbehave, you should ask Mom how Jack and I wrestled.

Mrs. Simms, I would like to know if you would agree to Patty and me becoming engaged while you are in Freeport. If you think it would be better to wait, we will understand. If it is alright, Dad and I have planned to buy the ring in Chicago on the twenty-third of this month. By now you must know how much Patty and I love each other. Mom and Dad realize that Patty is the only girl for their son. I know this is not the typical way to ask a girl's folks if I may marry their daughter, but you are aware that I am in a spot, being so far away and in the Navy. If you agree, do not tell Patty as I would like it to be a surprise.

That P.S. of yours said to take care of yourself. Now do you suppose I would let anything happen to me with a life like I have to look forward to? Believe me when I say that no matter what happens, as soon as the war is over, I will be coming back and then Patty's and my biggest dream will come true.

I am waiting to hear from you, and as I sit here I realize the next letter I receive from you will be the most important one in my life.

As ever,

Keith

Mother and Daddy must have agreed because Keith did give me the ring when we visited Freeport in April. At this time, Keith's family was living in a large Victorian home on Stephenson Street. It even had a ballroom. Keith's parents and friends entertained Mother and Daddy, and Keith's friends had parties for us.

On the night Keith gave me the ring, we had been to a party at the home of one of his friends. After the party, as we were driving away in his parents' car, I noticed a string of cars behind us. I wasn't certain they were following us, so I remained silent. Finally Keith stopped on a dark, gravel road. I am not able to recall the exact details, but I remember expecting a surprise gift, which he had mentioned in a letter. Just as he was preparing me for the surprise, a cohort of his knocked on the window. As Keith rolled down the window, the friend loudly inquired, "What did she say? We are anxious to know." I didn't quite understand what his friend had asked, but I had an idea. Not wanting to spoil the moment, I asked "What's wrong, Keith? What did he say?" Keith, fearing the mood may have been destroyed, replied with a touch of disappointment, "He wanted to know if I had given you the gift yet?" Then he gave me the ring saying, "Please say you love me enough to wear this ring and to become my wife after the war is over." I answered with a definite, "Yes," as he slipped the ring on my finger. What followed was a series of kisses, embraces and words of passion. The cold air in the car was warmed by promises of everlasting love and devotion. Neither one of us could have realized what our futures would be. We were only aware of what we felt for each other. Life could never again be as exciting, as exhilarating, or as complete; at least, that is how it seemed within that brief space, when nothing existed but the two of us.

Not long after our visit, Keith was transferred to the west coast. He boarded a troop train on April 20, 1945, and arrived at Shoemaker, California, on April 24. He was stationed at Treasure Island until he was assigned to the air craft carrier U.S.S. Cabot on May 4. As the Cabot had been damaged in previous battles, the overhaul at Hunter's Point was not completed until June. The carrier then left for Pearl Harbor, arriving there July 4. From Pearl, they journeyed across the South Pacific, en route for the invasion of Japan and the Wake Air Strike (August 1945). Then, after engaging in battle at Eniwetok, the Cabot headed for the Yellow Sea to support the landings of occupation troops in that area. Finally General Mac Arthur signed the treaty with Japan on the U.S.S. Missouri in Tokyo Bay on September 2, 1945. However, the Cabot remained in that vicinity until October 1945; at this point, the Cabot and crew began the return to the States. There was a letter Keith wrote a few days before the Cabot was ordered back to the States which vividly described a few of his experiences. Censorship had been lifted partially, so he was able to offer more detail of his activities and impressions.

September 14, 1945

Hi Honey,

I thought there were a lot of ships at Pearl Harbor, but you should see them here. There is everything from row boats to the largest air craft carriers.

There are still some "Nips," hiding in the mountains, who haven't surrendered yet. We were warned not to go out of bounds while on liberty for it is very dangerous. We were also warned not to fraternize with the Jap civilians who live in the villages. One of the most important reasons is they are afraid leprosy would break out among the men. The native women here will do anything for soap, cigarettes or clothes. When I say anything, I mean it. That is a touchy subject to write about, honey, but it is a problem here, so all personnel is warned to stay away from them.

Everyone is talking about where we will go next. Some say Tokyo, others say the Philippines, but, of course, everyone hopes it will be the States. No one knows for sure though, so there is nothing to do but wait.

I am afraid that every sentence I write, I shouldn't. You see they have just lifted censorship halfway and by that I mean they allow us to seal our own letters now, but still you are not to write where you are and where you have been. They have warned us they will open our letters at random. I know it is not worth the risk, but you have waited long enough without knowing where I've been. From now on you are going to be informed.

After I wrote you the letter saying I was in Okinawa, we went fifty miles off the coast of Japan. We were sitting out there waiting to go into Tokyo Bay, but something went wrong and instead we started for Korea, Mongolia, China and that part of the world. I couldn't begin to tell you about all of the sights I have seen. I remember one night, when it was almost dark, we ran into nearly a hundred junks (Chinese fishing boats). With my being up on top of the bridge and with a strong pair of glasses, I had a "bird's eye view." We did not change our course, and, before we knew it, we were in the middle of their fishing fleet. Their boats were all about us and some only a hundred yards away. When I looked through the glasses, it seemed as though I could reach out and touch them. I noticed one of them bowing up and down with the biggest grin on his face. I guess he was really glad to see us, after so many years under the rule of the "Nips."

Right now I am in Okinawa again, and, as I sit here on the gun mounts, I can see the "bloody" island off to the west about a quarter of a mile. So far we have had no liberty here, but I think we will start tomorrow. All I can tell you is that it is very mountainous. Maybe after tomorrow I can tell you more. We are supposed to stay here ten days. If this letter reaches you by September 24, you will know exactly where I am at the moment you are reading this letter.

Where we go from here, I do not know, but, as I said before, I will keep you informed. How I wish we would start back for the States.

I want to tell you, darling, just how much I love you, but I know I cannot put my feelings into words. You are the most perfect girl alive, and when I think I am lucky enough to have you for a future wife, I swell with pride.

Love and kisses,

Keith

On the way home, the carrier stopped at various islands to receive personnel who were returning to the States. The Cabot arrived in Long Beach, California, on November 9, then sailed for the east coast, by way of the Panama Canal. The carrier docked in Philadelphia on December 3, 1945. However, Keith was not issued his leave until the day after Christmas. While Keith was struggling to reach Charleston from Philadelphia, I was traveling home from Ward-Belmont College in Nashville, Tennessee, the school I attended after graduating from high school. But, before I continue with this saga, you will enjoy reading a letter Mother wrote to me, just before my taking the train home for Christmas vacation. This letter offers a deeper view of my mother and her mind set at this stage of her life. She was then thirty-six years of age.

December 14, 1945

Dear Patty,

This is really a Christmas day; snow is softly falling and everything is so peaceful, except for John and Dudley. John has a cold and so does Dudley, but not as bad as John's. However, neither one is ill enough for bed, but too ill for school. And, oh dear, I have to separate them every other minute.

That isn't what I wanted to say. I want to tell you to remember not to talk to anyone you don't know and please find the Charleston girls and stay with them all the way home. Bobbi [Keith's cousin] will be home Friday at five o'clock. We all are so excited. A big box came for you today from Chicago. I thought you and Keith might like to open it together. Tell Bev [my roommate] to have a nice trip home.

Oh, I almost forgot to tell you we have an invite to the Buford girl's wedding and reception on December 26 to Roy Sears. It is formal.

See you soon.

Love,

Mother

Watch your coat and purse. Be sure to have change and tell the conductor you want to change to the C&O at Covington [Kentucky]. Or so they told me. But, stay all together and watch your coat [my new beaver] and yourself.

As you probably have surmised, I made it home without being abducted or robbed, and in time for the engagement party our families had been planning for months. It would be the first time we had seen each other since we became engaged during the previous April. The party was held at my parents' home on December 20. While in Nashville, I purchased a long, white chiffon dress, embroidered with dark red sequins. The buffet was prepared by our favorite caterer. The house was filled with my family, Keith's family, and friends. However, the celebration was flawed, as Keith was not able to attend; the Navy changed his leave at the last minute, so there was no way to reschedule the event. The first date we had chosen was after Christmas; then the Navy refused to give him a leave at that date, so we changed it to before Christmas. Thinking that was a definite date, we made all the arrangements, but the Navy changed their decision once again. The war was over, but Keith's naval duty was not. His parents and his brother Jack served as representatives for him. It was a lovely party, but the excitement and sparkle of two young people in love was missing. Nevertheless, Keith arrived on December 27, in time to read the engagement announcement in the Sunday *Gazette.*

During this leave, Keith and I were able to continue our courtship in body, rather than by mail, phone, or prayers. I met Keith at the train station, with both of our families present, but their attendance did not hinder our display of love. He jumped off the train and immediately embraced me. He kissed my hair, my cheeks and my lips, while both of us were attempting to project verbally our happiness of being together once more. Keith and I have always enjoyed each other, and to this day, we respond physically to each other, even in the midst of turmoil. We may disagree on mundane affairs, but our sexual impulses and acts are separated from ordinary or routine experiences. God has truly blessed us with a gift of sexual happiness. However, both of us agreed and agree that the supreme act of love should wait until after marriage. God constantly proclaims true joy is found through total commitment to him. To sacrifice instant gratification by waiting until the ceremony of marriage has been held, declaring complete love and trust is difficult, but it is another way to reach paradise on earth and in heaven. Many times we were tempted to relent, but, realizing the cost, we chose not to pay the price. We often made wrong choices, but this was not one of them. To God be the praise! However, we do not condemn others who may disagree; this is our belief.

While Keith was in Charleston, we celebrated his nineteenth birthday. As a surprise, I gave him a gold ring set with a small diamond. I explained, "Darling, you deserve a ring with a huge diamond, so I am planning to replace the diamond with a larger one each year." Well, I lied. The diamond was not replaced until December 28, 1996, on our fiftieth anniversary.

And, the large box that Mother mentioned in her letter, instructing me how to protect myself, contained a lovely Queen Anne mahogany hope chest, from Keith. I have used it constantly, since removing it from the crate. I was surprised (though I shouldn't have been) that he was aware of what would please his bride-to-be. Once again he displayed a understanding of me and a desire to make me happy. Not many men would have chosen such a perfect gift for the one they loved. That chest still stands in our house, but the contents have changed through the years. In the beginning there were pillowcases, towels, tablecloths, and napkins, in preparation for our life together. Now it contains Christmas decorations, Keith's Navy gloves and belt, one original pillowcase, Tia's first ballet shoes, a book by Catherine Marshall and a huge Christmas card that Keith sent with the chest. Whoever inherits that chest will discover a composite picture of our marriage.

On the way back to Freeport from Charleston, Keith and his family spent the night in Gary, Indiana. After reaching his hotel room, he wrote to me.

January 3, 1946

Darling,

Just as always, I miss you so very, very much, my darling, as I have written so many times before. I just can't see why it has to be that I am not able to be with you all the time. I am sure that now there is no doubt in your mind just how much I do love you. I still cannot make myself believe that I have left you once again. Oh, darling, I hope so much I will be able to come to Nashville to see you, if I receive a twenty-day extended leave.

If I do not receive an additional twenty days, I wonder how long it will be before we are together again. Let's both pray that it will not be as long as the last time. Oh, honey, I love you so much. What a wonderful day it will be when we are married and will be able to spend every day of the rest of our lives together. Just think from that day on it will be Patty, Patty, and more Patty. No more Navy, no more trains, just you, day and night forever.

You know, honey, it's so wonderful to be in love. I mean having our hope chest, a start on our silver and whatever we will need after we are married. Speaking of perfect leaves, I have just spent one and the main reason it was perfect was because I spent it with a perfect girl. Oh, how I love that "gal."

It is getting rather late and Jack is yelling for me to turn out the light. Believe it or not, this is the last piece of paper left in the room. Always love me, Patty, and start praying once again, as I am going to do, for the days to pass quickly until we are together. I wish we were heading the other way and that I was arriving in Charleston, instead of Freeport, tomorrow.

Goodnight for now, sweetest, and never forget that Keith George is too much in love with you to do anything but always love, miss and want to be with you

Sweet dreams,

Keith

From Charleston, Keith went to Freeport and then back to Philadelphia. He returned to ship January 7, 1946. On January 9, he wrote me a letter that I must share with you. (I now feel that I am becoming close friends with whoever is reading these letters, and I am even acquiring a feeling of guilt whenever I omit a letter which is so full of meaning and veracity.)

January 9, 1946

Wonderful You,

Last night of all nights I was unable to reach you. I put my first call through to you at a quarter to seven and it went straight through. I reached Ward Belmont without delay but the line to your dormitory was busy, so the operator said that she could call me back in five minutes. In five minutes, she reported all the circuits to Nashville were busy and that there would be a one to two hour delay. I asked her what she took me for and told her that

I just heard her talking with the school. All she would say was, "I am sorry; would you like to try later." Oh, was I mad. If I could have gotten hold of her....

Another thing that happened last night was when I phoned in the telegram I sent to you. After I had finished dictating it to her, she asked, "Are you married?" I said, "No, why do you ask?" She replied, "Oh, I just wondered from what you said in the telegram: 'All my love, all my life.'" I then told her of our plans to marry as soon as possible. Then she said, "You sound as if you love her." I told her, "You bet your life. I have the sweetest girl alive (honestly)." She said, "She must be sweet." I asked her what she meant by that and she replied, "Well, I was on last night when you sent her a telegram and then again tonight. All I have to say is when a guy sends his girl a telegram every night, he must be in love." It seemed strange at the time because millions of people phone messages everyday.

There is one more question I want to ask you. Is there anything I do, any habits I have or just anything I say that you don't like? You see I am so terribly in love with you that I want to know. I can easily understand how there may be a few minor habits that could be corrected immediately. If there is and you tell me, I guarantee I will stop them. I don't know what brought that thought to mind. It is that you are so wonderful, and I want to be as near perfect for you as I possibly can. Understand?

I am so very much in love with you. If you only knew how I want to take you in my arms right now, this very minute, and kiss you like only I can. If this could only be a dream and I would wake up at your home in Charleston and find you waiting. I know it's silly how I write and write and say nothing, but as I said before, I have been in a dream with a dream since I first met you.

I am going to tell you something that is the real truth, so help me on my honor. Do you remember that morning I told you that you looked pretty and that you smelled so good? Well, you did, really, honey. If you don't stop doubting my words, I am going to keep my thoughts to myself from now on. Do you want to know why you looked so sweet? Well, I'm going to put you wise, whether you want to know or not. Now, this is straight from me, and I know there is something. I don't know exactly what it is, or I should say I can't put my finger on it. No matter what you are doing; no matter what time of the day or night it is; there is that something that is just plain wonderful. I have known many girls, but no other one in the world has that but you. Do you understand what I am trying to tell you, Patty? You have something no other girl has. You're Patty, you're Patty

Simms and believe me when I tell you that I couldn't ever begin to live without you.

Time to quit for now, baby, but I will be writing again tomorrow night, trying to explain to you how dearly I love you.

Always,

Keith

I reached Ward-Belmont about the same time Keith arrived in Philadelphia. After such a busy and wonderful vacation, I was depressed to return to the life of a student. To make it worse, Mother and Daddy were leaving for New York, as I was leaving for Nashville. How I longed to go with them! New York has always been one of my favorite places to visit.

Keith called me my first day back and Mrs. Collins (the dorm mother) allowed me to answer the phone, which was a miracle. I've suspected Keith said something exceedingly nice or kind or maybe both. He always seemed to phone when I needed him the most, and this was one of the times.

On Wednesday, Mother and Daddy had called me from New York before I left for a play. A friend of theirs was in the hotel room, so I talked to him too. He had a son who had been killed in Europe, and I was able to relate to his situation. While we were saying our good-byes, Mother and Daddy told me they were going to El Morroco and the Stork Club that evening. At that time of my life, I anticipated Keith and I would do the same thing in the future. As it happened though, Keith has never enjoyed large cities or clubs.

Keith called Mother and Daddy, on the same evening, and made plans to meet them in New York the next day. On Thursday night, he joined Mother and Daddy at their hotel and then went to Otto Becker's home for dinner. Mr. Becker was president of The Buying and Research Syndicate in New York in which Daddy was part owner. Then, at one o'clock in the morning, they took a tour of the Big Apple by taxi. This was the first time Keith had been in New York, and he was impressed. He saw Central Park, China Town, the Stork Club, the Waldorf, Delmonico's, and Times Square, among other sights.

By this time, Keith had been told he was being re-assigned, but he was not told where he was going. He was so disappointed. At the end of his letter that night, he wrote:

This is another one of those nights I feel so confused and mixed up. Gos.., it is a terrible feeling knowing tomorrow you are going somewhere and not knowing where. It wouldn't be so bad if I knew I would stay in the States, but do you realize they could and may send me to any place in the world. The only way to look at it is, if they do send me out again for a year or so, the next time I come back the chances are very good that I will stay in the States until I receive my discharge. I know it is difficult waiting for me so long, darling, but I think that you have stuck out the worse of it and won't have much longer to wait.

I was just thinking how terrible it would be going to sea without your love. The thoughts of you out there makes me want to live and come back. If you could only know what is inside of me and the feeling that my whole body has for you. Oh, Patty, why does it have to be, why can't I stay here? Why can't we be married and be happy as so many other people are. I can't see it. I can't seem to get it through my head that I may go a long time again before I see you. Please, darling, no matter what happens, believe I will come back. I think I had better bring this letter to a close before I start tearing this place apart. I have never felt like this before. Of course, when I said good-bye over the phone the last time, I talked to you from the west coast and I felt terrible but this time—Oh! Golly!

Hey, come on now, Harrison, you are letting your imagination run away. How do you know you might not be able to stay in the States? You might be able to see her within the next week. See what an affect you have on me, honey? You have gotten me to the stage where I have started talking to myself.

"Gotta" go now, sugar.

Forever,

Keith

By Sunday, January 13, the Navy had notified Keith that he was receiving a twenty-five day leave, and, when it was completed, he was to report to the Navy Pier in Chicago. He had no idea where he would go from there, but he hoped it wouldn't be one of the coasts because that usually meant an overseas duty. The problem now was deciding where we could meet and be together for at least part of his leave. Often we had planned on his coming to Nashville, yet we both realized I could not be released from school for long periods of time, even if Mother and Daddy came to Nashville also. In addition, Ward-Belmont was entering Dead Week (preparing for final exams) and following that was Exam Week. Fortunately, the school gave the students a break from classes after Exam Week, so with my parents' permission, I was able to fly to Chicago's Midway Airport where Keith would meet me; then we planned to drive to his parents' home in Freeport. Mother and Daddy were to arrive there by car on the same day.

The moment I stepped off the plane in Chicago, I felt the coldest wind I had ever experienced. My teeth immediately began to chatter, but, when I saw Keith waiting by the gate, the oddest thing happened; the cold air disappeared. Walking away from the plane, I remember dropping my luggage and running toward Keith. As we met, he reached forward and kissed me on the lips. I pressed my head into his neck, and we embraced. He whispered into one ear, "If you could only realize how often I have dreamed of our being together like this. I never want to let you go." Of course, we couldn't remain in that cold air forever; so, releasing each other, he retrieved my luggage and we started for the parking lot. Finding the car, we began our trip home to Freeport.

It wasn't thirty minutes, until Keith pulled the car to the side of the road, stopped the motor and placed his arms around me. Each time we were together seemed to be the first. He kissed my cheeks, my lips, my neck. Our bodies pressed together in happiness. Once more we were in each other's arms, where we belonged. God had answered our prayers.

"Keith, I can't believe that this is truly happening, that I am here with you, able to touch you, to feel you."

"It seems we have been apart for years instead of one month. I can't bear being away from you. You are always on my mind," Keith declared.

Turning slowly toward him, I said, "There is absolutely nothing we can do about this situation until you are discharged, and I pray it will be this summer. Then we will have a month together at Geneva Lake, before the college classes begin."

"Why can't we find a preacher and be married now, while you are here? No one would know, but I can wait, if you can. It would be wrong in a million different ways, yet wonderful, right?" Keith asked.

"Yes, it would be wonderful and exciting, but wrong. Even if we had enough time to obtain a license, we couldn't break our promises to our parents. They have trusted us; God has trusted us. We would be sorry for years to come."

Keith shrugged. "You are right, but I wish you weren't."

This was one of the few occasions that we had been completely alone; we sat in the car, sharing our love and enjoying just being together and touching each other. Finally, Keith placed the keys in the ignition, and we drove on to Freeport and to our waiting parents.

As I grow older, the past becomes more alive than the present. Some of my friends say they feel the same way. The past is something we understand and enjoy; perhaps we only remember what we choose to remember. I am not certain that's true, but, for me, remembering the past has brought moments of happiness.

While in Freeport, we often visited Krape Park, one of the many lovely parks located there. It was winter, so the trees were stripped of their leaves, but it didn't matter. Everything was perfect, as we had each other. One afternoon we were walking through the piles of leaves which had fallen on the rock-covered paths. We were building castles in the sky, creating plans for days to come, when we would be together for as long as we wanted. Keith stopped walking and drew me close to his warm body. He kissed me and I wrapped my arms around his neck and kissed him on the nose.

"Does your mother ever kiss you on the nose?" I asked

"Stop changing the subject," he said.

So, I did, and we continued walking. Both of us realized God was offering us the opportunity to enrich our relationship. After all, if we counted all the bits and pieces of time we had been together, it would have totaled a little less than a month. We had so much to learn about each other, and we were making the effort.

When we weren't alone, we were visiting his relatives or friends or going out to eat or to parties. We looked at the apartment we might rent from Baba (German for grandfather) after we were married. We even discussed expenses and income.

Warning me, Keith reported, "We won't have much money, but Baba wouldn't charge us very much rent anyway. Mom thinks it will be about fifteen dollars a month. That way we will be able to save money to build a house on the lot my parents are giving us as a wedding gift."

Our six days together ended on Thursday, February 7. We returned to Chicago with Mother and Daddy. I caught the plane to Nashville, Keith returned home on the train and Mother and Daddy drove back to Charleston. A few days later, the Navy sent Keith to the west coast to complete his duty, so he and I did not see each other again until July of 1946, when he was finally discharged.

Our families planned a reunion at Geneva Lake in Wisconsin. It was a perfect place for a young couple in love to prepare for a life together. The lake was spring fed, blue and clear, surrounded by gorgeous homes and cottages with boats at each dock. Each family rented a cottage on Belvedere Park, right by the lake shore. God even sent a moon; you see, God also knows I'm a moon person. Nothing is more beautiful or romantic than a ball of silvery white on a dark velvet sky. Our world became a soft dream of life. Nothing could break the spell created during those few weeks.

A month later I was asking myself to what world did our dream fly. Of course, it was gone forever, leaving us with a treasure of rich memories. To this day, Keith and I fervently attempt to visit that area in Wisconsin, at least once each summer. Just a day or two of being there renews our love, our faith in our life together and allows us to praise the Lord for the blessings he has offered us.

During the following winter, on December 28, 1946, we were married at the Baptist Temple in Charleston, West Virginia. My wedding dress and veil were designed by me and created by my great aunt. As Daddy had a yard goods business, we were able to buy Skinner bridal satin. The war had not been over long enough for production to return to normalcy, so it was difficult to obtain many of the items for the wedding. Mother, Daddy, and I traveled to New York to shop for my trousseau. My parents purchased for me a beautiful rose pointe lace collar and head piece from a shop which specialized in antique laces. Daddy ordered white kid gloves from France for the female members of the wedding party. The bridesmaids wore dresses of deep red velveteen, and my sister, who was my maid-of-honor, wore a dress of moss green velveteen. The bridal attendants carried matching muffs decorated with poinsettias. The reception was held in the ballroom at the Daniel Boone Hotel. That is one event Keith and I will always remember. Of course, we had planned the perfect honeymoon to equal the perfect wedding. We reserved a compartment on the C & O Railway to Richmond, Virginia, and then on the Orange Blossom Special to the Cloister Hotel at Sea Island, Georgia.

After the reception, Keith and I returned to "401" to dress for our trip to Sea Island. After all the months of waiting and preparing, we were anticipating our joy in being together and becoming one body of passion and affection. The wedding was everything we had thought it should be, but it was not without blemishes. Because Mother had been continuously voicing her doubts about our marrying, I decided to discuss the situation with our pastor, Dr. Austin. His being not only our religious leader and guide but also a close and beloved friend made him a well-qualified person from whom to gain wisdom. He understood my family, me, and the situation; thus, his agreeing to counsel me helped me to realize Mother would have objected to my marrying anyone.

Dr. Austin said to me, "Patty, it is not your marrying Keith; your mother never truly believed you would marry. The relationship between you and your mother has been extremely strong; therefore, she objects to your marrying anyone. She will always believe no man is right for you. Naturally, the decision is yours, but, if you wait to marry someone whom your mother approves, you will never marry."

So we proceeded with the wedding. Our family doctor helped Mother to fulfill her responsibilities by giving her an injection before the ceremony. The event was a warm and loving celebration, which could not have taken place without my mother's ideas and direction. I regret she was unable to be as ecstatic as Keith and I were.

Before leaving the house, to catch the train to Georgia, Keith and I were toasted with champagne by our family and friends. The ride to the train station was a mad rush of "well-wishers." Keith and I feared we would miss the train completely; after all, the Simmses were notorious for being tardy for departures. However, in the midst of advice, best wishes, congratulations, jokes, appreciation and tears, Keith and I climbed the steps to the train car. With thoughts of time alone and much lovemaking, we entered our compartment, but, as the porter had not followed the directions given to him, we were forced to wait at least thirty minutes longer. (At least, it seemed that long.) Finally, entering the compartment, we prepared ourselves for the night and climbed into bed.

Difficult as it may be to believe, by this time, Keith and I were mentally and physically exhausted. We decided the environment was not what we wanted as the background for our first complete act of love, the act for which we had waited two years, so we agreed to wait one more night. However, being our first time in a bed together, we undressed completely, covered ourselves with the sheet and blankets, turned off the lights, and embraced. First we whispered to each other.

Putting his hand around me, Keith asked, "Did you fall in love with me the first night we met?" (This is a question Keith has asked many times.)

Hesitating, I answered. "Well, perhaps not the first night, but soon after. After all, I wasn't certain you were honest about your feelings toward me."

"What did you like best about me?"

"Truthfully, your attention towards me, and daring to express yourself in front of your aunt and uncle and my parents and my sister and even you cousin. Weren't you a little nervous about what they would say?"

"I didn't care what they said. I knew I wanted you and hoped you wanted me."

Then we kissed and touched and lastly I turned over on my side. He placed his body against mine and we drifted off to sleep. Later I was reminded of a verse in the Bible: "Do not arouse or awaken love until it so desires" (Song of Songs 2:7b).

The next morning, we had to change trains at Richmond, Virginia. His Uncle Bob had given us money for our Sunday dinner, so we asked some local residents to suggest a restaurant and decided on this wonderful seafood establishment. This was not something new to us, as we had eaten alone before, but, nevertheless, it seemed different. I think both of us were slightly embarrassed but filled with bliss. We talked and laughed and enjoyed our first meal as a married couple.

About six o'clock, we caught the train going south to Darien. This again was a night trip, but, on this evening we were more rested and relaxed. The mood had changed, and we were ready to begin our life together as husband and wife. Although we hadn't been together a great deal, we had become acquainted through our letters and phone calls and even gifts. After Keith's discharge from the Navy, we spent six hectic months in the same town, planning the wedding, working, and going to Morris Harvey College. These months afforded us a period in which we were able to adjust to reality. The war had ended; life for everyone was returning to normalcy, whatever that was. In fact, everyone (including us) had to redefine life as it should be after a war. It was impossible to return to a place which no longer existed.

At last, at this moment, and with God's answering our prayers, we were in a bed in a compartment on a train headed for paradise, or that is what we expected. By now, we were experts at foreplay, but, my being a virgin resulted in our first complete act of love being somewhat difficult and trying. Neither one expected anything less than an explosion of rejoicing and passion, which finally did come to pass. We were discouraged but not defeated. The truth is we became so adept and successful at sexual interchange that, by the end of our honeymoon, I was pregnant. This certainly was more enjoyable than social interchange. God knew what he was doing when he created two different sexes.

Our first home was a small apartment on Washington Street, supposedly the longest block in the United States, or at least that was what I had always been told. Finding an apartment was difficult, as the service men were returning; thus, we found it necessary to offer a one hundred-dollar "reward." This was also a landlord's method of defeating the rent freeze. There was a bedroom and bath upstairs and a small living room and kitchen downstairs. It was comfortable and convenient to the bus line, which we needed as both of us were attending Morris Harvey College in downtown Charleston and we had no car. At that time, the college classrooms were located throughout the business area. We attended classes in the public library, Fruth School, and the St. Marks Methodist Church.

Keith worked at the Montgomery Ward store his Uncle Bob managed, and, when I was needed, I helped at the Piece Goods Shop. However, discovering I was pregnant, caused some of my activities to be curtailed. When the spring term was over, we left our apartment and traveled on the train to Freeport for the summer. Keith supervised the family stores while Mother Bee and Dad Harrison toured Canada and the northeast coast. We returned to Charleston in time for the fall term to begin. Keith had registered at Morris Harvey under the GI Bill (an act which changed the lives of many who had served during World War II, as well as the future of our country). Due to my delivery date drawing close, my life as a student temporarily ended. I was not disappointed, as being a "stay-at-home" wife and mother was what I expected to become, especially for now.

Tia was born in St. Francis Hospital on October 2, 1947. Mother and Daddy were in New York in body but in Charleston by voice, thanks to the services of the phone company. Dr. Summers, a family friend who lived two doors from "401," delivered Tia. During the birth, my Aunt Jackie sat at the hospital with Keith. When Mother and Daddy returned, they brought with them a private nurse, sheets and gowns from home and the decision that I was to remain in the hospital for two weeks. Mother explained, "It took your body nine months to arrive at this condition; please, give it two weeks to return to its previous condition." So I did, but it is obvious in the home movies taken, by the end of two weeks, I could barely walk.

Mother had purchased a hooded bassinet during a previous visit to New York and had decorated it with a satin lining covered with small bows in blue and pink. The outside was trimmed with embroidered organdy; a huge satin bow, fastened to the top of the hood, completed Tia's new bed. This was an indication of how all of our lives were to change.

Keith and I were living with Tia at "401," waiting to move into a cottage owned by Grandmother. In my opinion, the relationship between Mother and Keith and Grandmother immediately began to deteriorate due to each of them wanting to be an integral part of Tia's life. Grandmother, who had natural nursing talents, instructed me in the method of bathing, dressing and feeding a new baby girl. Mother felt she was to create a perfect schedule for her. And, Keith was so enamored with her, he wished to be free to decide for himself what he could and could not do. Keith has always been a "hands-on" father, which, at that time, was not the attitude of the typical father. Even our moving into our own home did not remedy the situation. In addition, Tia was the perfect baby in appearance and behavior. She did everything on schedule, as directed, and smiled prettily through it all, resulting in each admirer thinking he or she was the favorite.

When it came time for Tia's first public appearance, Keith was selling shoes at a local department store, The Peoples Store, on Capitol Street. Of course, that was the chosen location for her debut. Mother parked the car in front of the store. We then removed the carriage from the trunk. The carriage was aqua with white tires and metal spokes. Inside the carriage, we had placed the mattress, the pads, the percale sheets, the hand embroidered pillows, and the pale pink, satin quilt of silk, handmade by Yolanda of New York. The carriage and its accompaniments would have stopped the Macy Parade, and, with the appearance of Tia as the sole inhabitant, no one was safe from becoming a true Tia fan. I can not remember what I wore, but it was the proper costume for a mother, wheeling her masterpiece to be viewed. Everyone, including customers and clerks, gathered around Tia and her carriage. They exclaimed over her beauty and remarked, "She is so perfect that it is difficult to believe she is real." I was proud to claim, "This is the daughter to whom I have given birth."

Until after Christmas of 1947, we managed to remain in Charleston. In January of 1948, Keith transferred to Carthage College (a Lutheran school which during this period was located in southern Illinois). We leased an apartment that happened to be over the home of the dean of Men and his wife. However, moving to Carthage was not a wise choice because Keith had a problem with combining college duties and the responsibilities of marriage. Thus, after the spring term, we moved once again. This time to Freeport. We settled into a downstairs apartment of an old Victorian house owned by Baba, his grandfather. In early 1946, Keith had discussed with him our living there after we were married, and he agreed.

Therefore, we removed ourselves from Carthage and planted ourselves in Freeport. Keith and Baba worked diligently on redecorating the apartment. Originally it had been the first floor of a huge house. Not surprisingly, the rooms were immense and the ceilings high. There was a kitchen, dining room, living room, two bedrooms, one bath and two porches. It was the largest living quarters we had occupied since we had married. We even bought an automatic washer. Also, it was the first time I had lived in a place heated by coal. In West Virginia, my family used natural gas. For furniture, we moved some pieces from Charleston and others from family homes in Freeport. With these articles and the many lovely wedding gifts we had received (including a piano given to us by Mother and Daddy), we were ready to begin another phase of our life together.

This phase opened with a celebration of Tia's first birthday. Family and close friends were invited, including Mother Bee and Dad Harrison (Keith's parents), Nana and Baba Edler (Keith's maternal grandparents), Grandmother Harrison (Keith's paternal grandmother), aunts and uncles, Tia's godparents Ena and Stanley Guyer, Jack (Keith's brother) and my parents. Mother and Daddy, who adored Tia (as did everyone else attending), drove over five hundred miles from West Virginia to downtown Chicago, to purchase a three tiered cake they had previously ordered from the Stop and Shop bakery; then they drove an additional hundred miles to Freeport. Several days after the party, Tia and I returned to Charleston with my parents. The return trip required two days, as the road system was not as advanced as it is today and we were traveling with a baby.

Views of the scenery along the roads remain with me still. Northern Illinois's autumn was almost completed. Nearly all of the landscape was of farm houses and harvested land. Bundles of hay were tied and left for storage. Recalling the trip at this late date, I visualize traveling south through Illinois, and then east through Indiana, Ohio, and fifty miles into Charleston, West Virginia. I was so anxious to arrive at 401 Fairview Drive. During the trip, I had felt nauseated and tired. I assumed it was due to my being so busy in Freeport and perhaps contacting a light case of flu. I supposed Mother and Daddy were disappointed, as I did not talk with them as much as I usually did. I had always been very close to my parents, emotionally and physically. After all, they were only eighteen and nineteen when I was born. Some people speak of huge gaps existing between their parents and themselves; this was not the case with us. I can't remember having secrets. The fact is I felt a need to share my happy and sad experiences with them. An example of this is when Keith was serving in the Navy (1944-1946); we wrote to each other almost everyday. Just recently (some fifty-five years later), he discovered Mother often opened my mail and read his letters. I neither thought it strange nor did I care, but Keith thought it strange and he cares even now.

While I was visiting, I continued to feel ill, was quiet and lost my appetite. Not surprisingly, Mother and Daddy suspected I was unhappy; in reality, I was pregnant with Karry, our first son and second child. Taking into account what occurred during the trip and that visit, the idea of Keith and my returning permanently to West Virginia possibly emerged in the minds of my parents. Daddy, not realizing what the reactions or results would be, asked, "Opal, what do you think of our opening a shop in Huntington?" And, smiling, she answered, "Oh, that is a wonderful plan. Perhaps Patty and Keith would want to be a part of it." Empires and worlds have been created from less

4

Decisions

Following our visit in Charleston, Tia and I returned to Freeport. Needless to say, she missed her Daddy, and I missed my husband. About a month later, Thanksgiving 1948 arrived. Mother Bee and Dad Harrison prepared the celebration and invited Nana and Baba, Mother Bee's parents. Also attending were Jack (who still lived at home), Keith, myself, and beautiful Tia, the guest of honor.

It snowed on Thanksgiving Day, but I was the only one surprised. Everyone else was accustomed to it snowing during the fall season. Keith's parents were living in a stately Tudor home on Harvey Street, near the house where Keith had been raised. His mother prepared the dinner which was similar to what we served in West Virginia, except for the green beans that tasted as if they had been cooked for thirty minutes instead of three hours and were definitely not flavored with a ham hock. And, because there were a fewer number of people to share the feast, no outside help was necessary. As expected, Tia was the center of attention. Mother Bee asked her, "Are you enjoying your Thanksgiving Dinner?" Tia smiled, shook her head up and down and answered, "Yes, good," then pointed her spoon at her Grandmother Harrison. It was enough to send Tia's audience into rounds of applause and chattering. Any response by Tia was appreciated by all, including her mother and father. After the entertainment, Mother Bee and I washed the dishes, and Keith helped to place them in the cupboard. The rest of the day was quieter and more subdued than what I was accustomed to experiencing at home. After all, not even Tia could create as much commotion as a house full of lively and talkative guests.

Turkey Day in Illinois was decidedly more peaceful than one in West Virginia; no one could have disagreed with that observation.

The weeks between Thanksgiving and Christmas were filled with "family and friends" activities, as well as those at church. Keith's family had been members of the First Lutheran Church for four generations. Thus, as soon as we moved to Freeport, we joined a couples Sunday school class, and I began to sing in the choir. Though the services were more formal than those at the Baptist Temple in Charleston, I enjoyed being with family, celebrating the coming of Jesus's birthday, and praising God.

During our autumn visit to West Virginia, it had been arranged for Keith, Tia and me to travel by train to Charleston for Christmas 1948. At this point, Keith and I were positive we were expecting a second child. Frankly, we had not planned the conception, but it was a happy event. There would be twenty months between the children, and having a sibling would be a pleasant experience for Tia. Also, Keith was a man who expected and wanted to be an active father. He had been involved with Tia's care in every way and was anticipating another addition to our family. However, our parents did not express the same reaction. "I am not surprised, but I do think you should have waited until Tia was at least two years old before having another child. It will be a problem physically and financially," Mother responded when hearing our announcement. Daddy did not disagree with Mother, but he considered the birth of another child our responsibility. Both of Keith's parents had attitudes similar to my father's. And, so we departed for Christmas holidays in West Virginia, anticipating an exciting visit. What we did not considered was the effect this visit would have on us and our family forevermore.

Arriving in Charleston, we found the Christmas season and spirit had begun. The house looked like one of those which appeared in *House Beautiful* magazine. Mother was jubilant, as this was her favorite season and everyone, including Tia, was at home for the festivities. Santa had brought a small red piano for Tia and even a dress which complimented it. The dress was white pima cotton smocked with red thread. Mrs Santa had purchased it at Sak's Fifth Avenue. (I have a photograph of Tia seated under the tree by the piano.) Tia was the perfect girl for the perfect house. Also, my sister Betty Lee was home for Christmas vacation from Ward Belmont Junior College in Nashville, Tennessee. Betty was two years younger than I, and we had been best friends and best sisters since her birth in 1929. We had even shared the same room until I left for college in the fall of 1945.

On January 5, 1946, while I was at home packing to return to school in Nashville, Betty (who was in a room near-by) wrote a letter to me that depicted the relationship existing between us.

Dearest Patty,

Well, you are in your room packing. I really hate to see you leave again, but there is nothing I can do. Besides, I guess I must become accustomed to your coming and going as you will be living in Freeport after you marry Keith. I hope you had a nice time here at home, but, of course, I know you did. It was wonderful having a sister with me again each and every day.

The time before your next break won't seem long for you as you will probably have many visitors during the next few months. Don't forget to keep your good grades as we are so proud of them (and you too).

I am not very good at writing letters, but you know I will miss you until we meet again.

All my love,
All my life,

Your loving sister,

Betty Lee

P.S. I may get a little mad at you sometimes but you realize I really love you, don't you?

Now, three years later, Betty Lee was a third year student at Ward-Belmont. During the fall, she had met a young man from Mount

Pleasant, a small town near Nashville. His name was Jim Jones. As his two sisters were attending Ward-Belmont, they had met Betty Lee and had decided to introduce Jim to her. It was evident their relationship was more than friendly. He was tall, good looking, pleasant and mannerly. However, his greatest attribute was loving horses almost as much as Betty did. She had always possessed an affection for horses, while I, on the other hand, had a fear of all animals, except the human ones.

During one summer vacation, while Betty and I were in high school, we attended a riding camp. I had no choice, but Betty invited the opportunity. One of the required activities was grooming the horses. That was a true lark; if it hadn't been for the aid of my sister, I would have escaped to the hills. The closing event was a horse show, complete with top hat, black riding jacket and boots. Betty Lee rode a gorgeous horse named Patricia Stonewall. I rode the slowest horse available and the nearest to the ground. To end the torture of this tale, I shall quickly announce Betty Lee won first prize and I fell off my animal. (I am not even certain it was a horse.) Mother and the instructor then insisted on my mounting the horse again and riding at least once around the ring. They declared, "You must ride this horse at least one more time so you won't be frightened when you ride again." Well, I rode one more time, but that was my last experience of traveling on the back of a live horse. Since then, I have admired horses at races, in barns, at circuses and in horse parks. Betty Lee, nevertheless, continued her avocation as a horsewoman until she died in 1991. The fact is she received an equestrian associate degree from Ward-Belmont in 1950. Her talents lay in sports, mine in the academic area.

Betty Lee did marry Mr. Jones in June of 1950; however, their love for horses appeared more enduring than their love for each other. They divorced a year later. Betty then returned to Charleston and earned a bachelor's degree from Morris Harvey College (now The University of Charleston) and married again in 1953 to John (Jack) Sears. Jack and she had three children: John, Tracy and Brent. Sadly, this marriage also failed, and Betty never again attempted to marry. I felt that Betty and

Jack were like two chemicals, which were not soluble. When mixed, the result was an explosion, not a compound. In addition, they "partied" a great deal, an activity which is detrimental to even a successful union.

Betty Lee was drinking even more during 1970 and 1971, the period of the suit. She and I had decided to give our Grandmother a joint Christmas gift, so I had mailed her a check to cover my part of the cost. After Christmas 1970, she mailed a note to me.

Patty,

Keep this check. It is only money stolen from Daddy by your no good husband thief. Grandmother wouldn't want it either.

Betty Lee

P.S. The S.O.B. won't let me talk to you on the phone. He is using drinking as an excuse. It won't work. He did it to Mother!

I can't say I wasn't affected by Betty's note, but not as much as most people would have imagined. I did not believe the note truly expressed what she felt. I knew she had been drinking; however, even a teetotaler would have been tempted to use alcohol during this period. Betty had to be confused over how I was reacting to the situation as I had decided not to discuss the suit in depth with Daddy, Mother or her. I didn't want them to be placed in judicative positions. Naive as I was (Some people may say stupid.), I had believed that when the suit was over, no matter what the decision was, our relationships would return to their initial stage. I said to myself, "After all, it is just money; money has no true value for our family. Nothing is worth as much as our love for each other."

In addition, I wasn't Betty's only problem. Betty and Jack were in the midst of a divorce, which was finalized later in 1971. The settlement was extremely emotional and demeaning to her. Jack possessed ample financial assets, so money was not a problem. And, as they had lived in the Sears family home during their entire marriage, the house remained his; however, he was also given custody of the children. Betty Lee was awarded an initial settlement, alimony and a convertible, which Jack had given her previously. Of course, she was destroyed. All of this happened during the period of our alienation, after the settlement of the PGS suit, so I was neither told all the details nor have I ever investigated the complete situation.

By the time our relationship was reinstated, Betty was manager of a Piece Goods Shop in the South Hills area of Charleston and had begun a new life for herself. Yet, it was not until July 21, 1974, that she had her last drink. The next day she left to receive counseling at Fellowship Hall in Greensboro, North Carolina; on her return, a month following, she commenced attending Alcoholic Anonymous meetings with a dear and true friend. Several years later she began a successful and enjoyable career in real estate and was involved in it until her death. Finally she had given God control of her life and her soul. On her marker is written the words, "This too shall pass," a truism with which most of us would agree.

Our reward is the love which continues. Betty Lee is constantly with me in mind and spirit. Each day when I talk to God, I pray for her and her family. God truly blessed me when he allowed us to become sisters, and I am looking forward to our reunion after my death. Now, after offering a deeper understanding of the relationship between my sister and me, my story again returns to Christmas Season 1948 in Charleston.

Christmas was not the only important event in December. Keith and I were married on December 28; Mother and Daddy's anniversary was December 29; Keith's birthday was the same day as my parents' anniversary, and then came New Year's Eve. Yet, even though there were special events and parties the entire season, there was also time enough to discuss business. During this period, Mother and Daddy offered us an opportunity to return to West Virginia, as they were planning to open a PGS in Huntington. It was to be a corporation.

Daddy explained to Keith, "This will be a partnership between you and me." Then Keith asked the obvious question, "How much will a partnership cost? You must know we have no available money at this time. We can barely pay our living expenses." Daddy replied, "Well, we have taken that into consideration. We are willing to offer you a partnership, if you are willing to move to Huntington. We believe a store in Huntington will do well as that area appears to be expanding in population and growing economically." Following this, Keith and I both expressed our gratitude for being given such a promising opportunity. Keith continued, "It is so kind of you to consider us for this position in the Huntington Piece Goods Shop. With a new baby expected, we will need a larger home and more money for expenses. Of course, we will have to think about it and discuss the idea with my parents. Dad has always assumed I would help him with the stores, and he is not as well as he used to be. His diabetes is growing worse. I must see what they think. When do you have to know?" Daddy answered, "I would appreciate knowing in about two weeks. We want to begin looking for a location and decide on the decorating. Actually, I would like to open it by spring. Just tell me as soon as you are able to talk with your parents."

After arriving in Freeport, Keith and I discussed the issue with his parents. Keith asked, "What do you think we should do about this? Patty and I know you have been expecting me to stay in the grocery business, and we realize it will be a great disappointment. We also know how much you will miss Tia. We think it's only fair to discuss this with you before deciding whether to go or stay." Keith's father responded, "This is something you must decide for yourselves. Of course, we'll be disappointed, but, at this time, the opportunities with the Simmses appear more promising than those of Harrison's Finer Foods. If you decide to leave, I will probably close the stores in a few years as Jack (Keith's brother) has no interest in them. The newspapers are filled with reports of supermarket chains moving into areas and destroying the small, home-owned grocery stores." Shortly after this conversation, Keith and I returned to our apartment. The next morning, we called my parents and accepted their enticing proposal.

Of course I was excited about returning to West Virginia. I missed the hills, the trees, my family, and the warmer climate. I also considered the future, as did Keith. I realized it was a sacrifice for him. In addition, there were times my mother and he had argued violently. As I previously mentioned, one reason for this was related to both Keith's and Mother's desire to do so much for Tia. Tia was the first grandchild and a girl. My mother loved babies and especially girls; according to her, they were inclined to be more calm, more affectionate, and more cuddly. In 1949, my brothers John and Dudley were twelve years old. Mother had repeatedly declared, "I should have had the twins first, when I was younger and had more energy." Truthfully, there were times when she would vent, "I don't know how to handle boys." She couldn't receive much advice from her mother, who had given birth to three females, or from Daddy, who had eight female siblings.

Yet, there was another reason for these disagreements between Keith and Mother. I had always been very close to Mother. She enjoyed doing what I did, and I enjoyed being with her. I continuously attempted to be what my parents wanted me to be. I felt they knew what was best. In fact, if Mother had not approved of Keith, I don't think he and I would have had a life together. She was the one who called me from the country club on that fall day in 1944 to say, "After we finish eating, your Daddy and I are bringing Clara and Bob Harrison to the house. They have with them their daughter Roberta and their nephew Keith who is here from Illinois." As I had been sitting with the twins and studying, I attempted to discourage her; but she ordered, "Patty, I want you to change your clothes and be ready to come downstairs." So I dressed and descended the steps about the same time they walked through the door. Keith asked me to marry him on our second date; I thought he was flirting. As fate had it, we became engaged about seven months later, but only after our parents had met and visited; even his Grandmother Harrison and Great Aunt Margaret came to West Virginia. Of course, they were also visiting Keith's Uncle Bob and his family who were living in Charleston at this time.

Remembering past events, I believe the relationship between Mother and Keith had really begun to deteriorate when our wedding date was decided in 1946. By December 1948, the time of the PGS proposal, I felt they were tolerating each other. We knew she wanted us to come home, though she hadn't said so. This was probably due to her knowing Keith did not approve of her strong influence on my making decisions. However, Huntington was fifty miles from Charleston. Isn't it a blessing we humans are not aware of future events? Yet, probably neither Keith nor I would have accepted such knowledge for hope often tends to blind our vision.

PART III

o o o o o o o o o o o o o o o o o o o o o o o o o o o o o o o o

He sits down with holy fears
And waters the ground with tears;
Then humility takes its root
Underneath his foot.

—Verse 3
"The Human Abstract"
by
William Blake, 1974

5

Deposition by Keith Harrison

One of the first problems to be solved, after deciding we had no choice but to respond to the suit, was selecting a law office to defend Keith. We had a close friend who was general secretary of the American Bar Association in Chicago. He suggested Keith's contacting the law firm of Huddleston, Bolen, Beatty, Porter and Copen. They reviewed the case and offered to accept it on a contingency fee. Attorney Michael Perry, a junior officer, was placed in charge.

The depositions were taken on March 10, 1971, in the First Huntington National Bank Building on Fourth Avenue. Keith's deposition was recorded first. The suit was brought by Dudley L. Simms (Daddy), Dudley L. Simms III (my brother), John L. Simms (Dudley's twin brother and my brother) and the Piece Goods Shop, Inc., against Keith G. Harrison. Neither John nor Daddy was present for Keith's deposition, only Dudley III. William C. Payne (one of Daddy's lawyers) interrogated Keith. The presentations of the depositions presented here were excerpted by me (Patricia Harrison) from copies of the depositions presented to Keith after the interviews were completed.

Mr. Payne began with the usual questions concerning name, address, time lived in Huntington, wife and children's names. By this date we had five children: Tia (now married), Keith Jr. (Karry), Scott, Sean, and Dirk. Next the relationship between Keith, Daddy and my brothers was established. Finally, the time period when the discussions occurred between Daddy and Keith regarding his coming to West Virginia from Freeport was examined. The dates determined were the months of December 1948 and January 1949. At the conclusion, it was obvious that arrangements were made during family conversations, not in formal meetings. Lawyer Payne requested, "I want you to tell us, if you will, Mr. Harrison, what was said in those conversations by both you and Mr. Simms, Sr." Keith asked, "This would of course be pertaining to the Huntington store?" Mr Payne answered, "Well, on all subjects." Keith then, attempting to answer, said, "Well, I imagine there was—the other part of the conversations was probably just. you, you know, 'How is the family?' and 'How is Tia?' and this type of thing. Pertaining to the store, he asked me if I would be interested in moving to Huntington to go into partnership with him, and, if I would be, that he would build the store or create a store in Huntington."

Mr Payne: "What kind of store?"
Keith: "A yard goods retail outlet."
Mr. Payne: "Did you agree to do this?"
Keith: "Eventually, yes, sir."

Next Mr. Payne asked Keith what the relationship was to be between him and the store, "if anything." Keith replied, "Well, that I was to be part owner of it, and we were to go in as partners together. I was under the impression while I was in Freeport that it was going to be on a fifty-fifty basis; that each was going to own half."

Mr. Payne: "Why did you have this impression?"
Keith: "Well he used the word 'partner' and—"
Mr. Payne: "And the word implies fifty-fifty to you?"
Keith: "Yes"

Following this, Keith was questioned further about any percentage being discussed. Keith answered that percentage was not discussed at this time; however, a partnership was.

Another important feature was Keith's role in the store, according to Daddy. Keith, expanding his responses, stated Daddy told him that he would be responsible for the management of the store, be a partner, and do the required daily activities. The next question posed by Mr. Payne was pertaining to capital. Was there any discussion in respect to his investing capital in the venture? Keith responded, "Never. No." Keith continued his answer by saying, "Well, you say was there any discussion. Certainly there was discussion, because he knew I had no money to invest and he told me that, if I would come to West Virginia, he had the money to invest and that I had the time to invest and that if we would move down and I would leave the business I had in Freeport, I would—you know, I would have, I thought, half of the business."

This point was key to the plaintiffs' case, and it was obvious by the line of questioning. Mr. Payne pursued the questioning by asking how it was possible for Keith to become an owner without any discussion of capital being invested by him. Keith reiterated that this was a gift to him.

◆   ◆   ◆

Reading the depositions some thirty years later has become a revelation. There are so many intents that I failed to notice or recognize at the time of the depositions. Of course, as I was not actually present, I relied on Keith's review and the court's typed recording. Taking this into consideration, it is possible I did not analyze the record as carefully as I am doing now. Thinking back, I just wanted the whole affair to end and our lives to continue as they had been. Of course this did not happen.

◆   ◆   ◆

The interview continued with Mr. Payne investigating Keith's experience and qualifications for becoming designated owner/manager of the Huntington PGS. He questioned Keith about the grocery stores and his responsibilities there. It was an attempt to debase Keith's previous responsibilities and activities. At least this is my view now. In 1949, it seemed as if everybody wanted us to move to Huntington and believed Keith would be competent in that position at the new store. No one needed to remind us we were young. We knew that, but we had considered youth an advantage. As a boy, Keith had worked in his father's stores, and I had helped Daddy in the Charleston shop since I was ten years old. A strange observation is his brother never wanted to work in the stores and neither did my sister. John and Dudley were really too young at that time. I remember working behind the pattern counter and adding the sales tickets. When I was in high school, Daddy took Mother to Florida as she was ill, and I was left in charge of checking the day's sales and making the deposits. I felt proud to receive such an important responsibility. Keith entered the Navy in 1944 and served on the aircraft carrier U.S.S. Cabot in the South Pacific. He was serving in the China Sea when MacArthur signed the treaty with Japan. This does not relate directly to retailing, but it does display tenacity, discipline, loyalty, and a sense of responsibility.

The questioning then led to our moving to Huntington in January of 1949. In actuality, we moved from Freeport to Charleston, as the Huntington store did not open until April. Our furniture and other objects were moved by van. The moving company packed the dishes, pans, utensils and even the clothes that we would not need until spring. Keith and I filled the suitcases, took Tia and left on the train for West Virginia. We stayed at Mother and Daddy's until March. During this time Keith trained at the store in Charleston, visited the shops in Beckley and Bluefield, and helped prepare the Huntington PGS for opening day. I would often come to Huntington with him as we were decorating our new home, which Mother and Daddy had chosen and secured for us by paying the money required for the down payment. We were so pleased with the house. No one had ever lived in it, and it was similar to a house Keith's family had built in the thirties. (He had grown–up in that house.) We then made the payments each month until the mortgage was cleared. We remain in that house until this day; we have made additions and changes, but we have never moved. I considered it one of our better investments.

The deposition continued with defining Daddy's role in the management of the store. Keith responded, "He was to advise me on—well, he was just to help me in any way that he thought, you know, was necessary in the buying and selection of fabrics and in advertising in the newspapers, and window decorating, and just everything that would pertain with the business." Next Mr. Payne posed an extremely important question.

Mr. Payne: "Do you recall a corporation by the name of The Piece Goods Shop Inc. being organized in the year 1949?"

Keith: "To the best of my knowledge, yes sir."

Mr. Payne: "What did you have to do with that, if anything?

Keith: "Well, I have always been under the impression that I had 40 shares in it and I was the Vice President of it."

Mr. Payne: "Did you or Mr. Simms, Sr. contact the person who prepared the papers for the corporation?"

Keith: "Mr. Simms."

Mr. Payne: "Did you attend any conference at any attorney's office at the time this corporation was organized?"

Keith: "I did not."

Mr. Payne: "Was this corporation we have just referred to the corporation which was to operate the Huntington Store?"

Keith: "To the best of my knowledge."

Mr. Payne: "Do you recall signing the statement of incorporation for this company?"

Keith: "I recall signing various different papers when I first came down here. There were several or numerous different ones. I was under the impression that the papers that I signed at that time were these papers, yes."

Mr. Payne: "What did you understand the effect of these papers to be in respect to you?"

Keith: "That these were the papers that made me 40 per cent or 40 shares owner of the business."

The next line of questioning was directed toward stock certificates. Mr. Payne asked Keith if he had received a stock certificate. Strange as it appeared and appears, Keith had received none because Daddy had said the certificates would be kept in the Charleston office, in the safe there, as it was the home office and there was not a safe in the Huntington PGS. The insurance papers, the contracts with different companies—all company papers were kept in Daddy's office in Charleston. As would be expected, Mr. Payne asked if he had ever received a stock certificate from the corporation proving his ownership. Keith replied that at the onset of the PGS he had signed many papers, and he thought the certificate ownership papers were included; however, he kept no papers as they were to remain in Charleston. Following this, Mr. Payne suggested perhaps Keith was merely a subscriber to shares of stock in the corporation. Keith replied, "I assume, yes, that anything would be possible, but I think it would be highly improbable, because I had all the faith in the world in Mr. Simms, and I am sure he would not have said 'this is something' or 'that is,' and then it wouldn't be, because I trusted him like I did my own dad."

Lawyer Payne nimbly attempted to connect Keith with being a subscriber who would receive stock upon payment of a consideration for the shares. Mr. Huddleston interceded and objected to the question, as Keith's lawyers did not agree with the legal conclusion and wanted their opinion recorded in the deposition. Mr. Huddleston conceded that a subscriber is one who enters into a contract with a corporation which obligates the corporation to issue shares of stock to the person upon payment of a consideration of shares. However, he insisted that the payment or money does not have to come from the subscriber. A side arrangement could exist where the corporation could put up the money and the subscriber would perform the services. Finally, Mr. Payne presented a true copy of the certificate of the corporation of The Piece Goods Shop Inc.. The certificate was signed by the State on June 25, 1949. It was verified by the Secretary of State John D. Rockefeller IV on December 15, 1970. Keith's signature was also on the document. At this point, Lawyer Payne emphasized that the certificate had been signed, but Keith was not able to produce evidence of his ownership. However, Keith had previously stated the stock was kept in the Charleston office as Daddy wished.

Following this, Mr. Payne asked Keith what statements Daddy made to him at the signing of the organization papers. Keith explained he was puzzled over the division of shares. (Daddy had 59 shares, Keith 40 shares, Mother 1 share.) Keith asked, "Dad, how come Mother is in that for 1 percent?" Daddy replied, "Well, because we need to have three different people to make this type of business." Keith did not know the difference between an incorporation and a partnership, but he did add, "It runs in my mind that he said, 'This is the best way to do it,' or he might have told me why it wasn't a partnership."

Further questions dealt with Keith being Vice President, his receiving a salary and a bonus, how much responsibility he had, and what functions Daddy performed after the shop opened.

◆   ◆   ◆

I will never forget the summer of 1949. If it were not the warmest summer ever recorded, it was nearly the warmest. We had opened the shop on April 29, a day before John and Dudley's twelfth birthday. Karry was born on June 11, 1949, in Charleston. I wanted him to be delivered there so I would have the same doctor, Dr. Summers, as I had with Tia. He was a neighbor of my parents and a close friend. So, after we were released from the hospital, we remained at my parents' home for a few weeks. Keith would commute by bus from Huntington to Charleston each evening and return the next morning to work at the

PGS in Huntington. Around the first of July, we decided we were ready to renew living in our own home.

In 1949, having air conditioning in a private home was rare; our only method for cooling the environment was the use of fans. Also, as neither the landscaping nor the lawn had yet matured, the outside of the house was surrounded by dirt, hay and a small amount of grass; there wasn't even a shade tree. In addition, telephone lines were difficult to obtain, causing us to be without a phone for several weeks into July. If there was an emergency, I would go to a neighbor's house to use the phone. And, we had no automobile. Praise the Lord, bus service was dependable, a half a block away. Also, taxis were easily obtained. In fact, we took a taxi to church. During that summer, Daddy often came to visit the shop, and, if he needed more time, he would stay over night with us. It felt strange to attempt to prepare his breakfast. Of course, I knew what he was accustomed to having for breakfast, and I strove to present him with a morning experience that would satisfy his usual expectations. As I recall, he was always pleased and appreciative. In fact, the emotion I felt as his Buick disappeared down the narrow brick street in front of our house is not yet forgotten. I was happy when he came and sad to see him leave.

When Daddy came, he would review the procedures at the shop, but Keith was in charge of the day–to–day operations. Sometimes, Keith would go over to the Watts–Ritter Wholesale House on Third Avenue to replenish the basic stock, but most of the buying was accomplished by a buying and research syndicate in New York, by Daddy on the phone or during a trip planned just for the purpose of buying. During the twelve years we were in the shop, Keith was invited just one time. Though Keith thought this odd, he didn't appear to resent his not being included.

There is a task my father claimed as his own; he enjoyed marking the remnants (short pieces of fabric left on the end of the bolt). These short pieces were removed, folded, marked with the yardage and the original price, and stacked to wait for Daddy to write the reduced price with his red pen. This may appear strange, but, as long as he was able to work in the PGS, he marked the remnants. Closing my eyes, I am able to visualize his standing at the back counter, puffing on his cigar, and preaching, "The profit is in this remnant."

◆　　　◆　　　◆

Mr. Payne: "What is your present occupation, Mr. Harrison?"

Keith: "I am employed by the City of Huntington."

Mr. Payne: "In what capacity?"

Keith: "I work in the License and Tax Division."

Mr. Payne: "When did you leave the employ of The Piece Goods Shop, Inc.?"

Keith: "February of 1961."

◆　　　◆　　　◆

February of 1961. A day of infamy. Daddy had come to the Huntington PGS with some of the clerks from Charleston, including Mrs. Parsons, an employee who had worked and managed the Charleston PGS. We had known each other for years. Our clerks, Keith and I, and the crew from Charleston took inventory and cleaned. Daddy had led us to think the shop would be closed. The financial condition was bad. The stock was low and the accounts were not paid. Daddy advised Keith to leave while he could do it graciously. There had been discussions between Daddy, Keith, and myself about conditions at the shop. Money had been invested more than once, and Daddy was not interested in continuing. Before, when there were problems, he would suggest solutions, but this time he was not interested. He said," I don't know. I have enough trouble of my own. Quite frankly, we will just close it down, and close it up." Finally he stopped coming, quit calling, and ignored the situation. After many prayers, sleepless nights, oceans of tears, and even research with knowledgeable people, Keith decided to do what Daddy had suggested. As we locked the doors, I inquired, "What about the shares?" Keith responded, "We still have them. I can't see how they will be worth anything but they belong to us."

◆　　◆　　◆

Mr. Payne: "Why did you leave the store?"

Keith: "Because he told me the store was no longer to exist, and he was going to bankrupt it. He was going to close it down."

Mr. Payne, "Didn't he tell you about this time that in his view you didn't own any stock in this company?"

Keith: "He did not. He has never told me that."

Mr. Payne: "Didn't he tell you at this time that the stock had never been issued?"

Keith: "He did not."

Mr. Payne: "What did you think the effect would be on your stock, of what was going to happen to the store?"

Keith: "Well, I didn't think—if the store was no longer in existence, I didn't think the stock—that the shares would no longer exist."

Mr. Payne: "From January 1961 on, have Dudley Simms, Sr., Dudley Simms III, John Simms, or the corporation itself, The Piece Goods Shop, Inc., done anything which indicated to you that any of these parties considered, that they recognized that you had a stock interest?"

Keith: "Yes, sir, they certainly have. They came to me with a piece of paper asking me to sign my shares to them."

Mr. Payne: "Was there anything else?"

Keith: "Oh, yes. Yes. Repeated visits to the house, discussing this. And threats, accusations and phone calls."

Mr. Payne: "You say you had a conversation with someone about your stock. Now, what are you referring to?"

Keith: "The stock in the Piece Goods Shop."

Mr. Payne: "Who was the conversation with?"

Keith, "With Dudley Simms, III."

Mr. Payne: "When was it?"

Keith: "I had one Christmas Day, and I had one Christmas Eve."

Mr. Payne: "What year?"

Keith: "It would be December of last year. The night of the twenty-fourth of December 1970. And then December 25, Christmas Day. And then we had—what was it?—three other conversations over at the house?"

Dudley Simms, III: Two others.

"Two others."

The following line of questioning dealt with conversation or correspondence concerning Keith's ownership of stock during the period from January 1949 until Christmas Eve 1970. Keith said it would be difficult to ascertain this in its entirety because of the amount of people involved and the number of years, but there were numerous ones. However, in 1949, John and Dudley were just twelve. By 1961, the year the shop was to close, John and Dudley were involved in the shops. At this time, John and Dudley were twenty-four, and, when the Huntington PGS was reopened, Dudley III was placed in charge; however, ownership was not discussed with us. At this point, Mr. Payne attempted again to prove that Keith had never owned the shares, but this time he asked Keith if he had ever shown ownership of stock in the Piece Goods Shop, Inc. on a loan application. I believe the idea was to show Keith had never listed the shares as assets; thus, he must not have truly considered the shares his. As this line of question led nowhere, Mr. Payne returned to the conversation at Barbara and Dudley's home on Christmas Eve 1970. Keith repeated the account of Dudley asking Keith to sign a piece of paper, which Dudley said Daddy wanted him to sign. Dudley claimed not to know what was written on the paper; he called it a technical or trivial thing. Reading the note, Keith recognized it was the release of his 40 shares. Keith then stated, "I am sorry, but I cannot sign it."

Mr. Payne: "Were you offered any money for it?

Keith: "I was not."

Mr. Payne: "Do you recall a conversation on Christmas Day 1970 with Dudley Simms, III?"

Keith: "Yes, sir."

Mr. Payne: "What exactly did you say to him on that date?"

Keith: "Well, that day our conversation was much more lengthy than it had been Christmas Eve. And I cannot be as implicit or as exact on that conversation as I was on Christmas night, but again it was pertaining to the 40 shares. But it was a little bit more in length and a little bit more in detail, this conversation. I think that we talked about why I felt I should not sign them over, and what my reasons were, and this type of conversation."

Mr. Payne: "Didn't you tell him on occasion that you feared the statue of limitations of some time period had elapsed on your claim against the company?"

Keith: "I said that?"

Mr. Payne: "Yes."

Keith: "No, sir. Or if I did, I don't remember it."

Mr. Payne: "Well, didn't you refer to the fact that you had been a long time in asserting your claim against this corporation?"

Keith: "I never asserted a claim against the corporation."

Mr. Payne: "Didn't you make the statement that you thought there was a question of whether or not your claim was still alive?"

Keith: "No. How would I have had that kind of knowledge?"

Mr. Payne: "Did you on the occasion make the statement to Dudley Simms III that you thought you should have signed something when you left the store? Just like you signed when you started?"

Keith: "No."

(A short recess was held)

After the recess, Mr. Payne asked Keith questions about his applying for a loan and not receiving it. Keith had applied for a loan on a car, but he was not asked to list his assets as no loans were being made on a car that old. Mr. Payne then pronounced an end to the examination, and Mr. Perry asked Keith a few questions.

Mr. Perry: "Mr. Harrison, did Mr. Simms ever indicate or tell you that everything that had to be done was completed to consummate your agreement at any time?"

Keith: "You mean in the beginning of the...."

Mr. Perry: "At any time."

Keith: "Well, I feel reasonably sure that he did, yes. There would have been no reason for me to doubt anything. I might have said, 'Are you sure it is all right, sir?' and he might have said, 'Keith, this is what we need to do and should do, and I have to have you sign these papers.' Yes, in my mind everything had been consummated legal and proper and everything else."

Mr. Perry: "But did Mr. Simms ever tell you everything had been completed should be?"

Keith: "I am sure that he did. I would have no reason to believe that he did not."

Mr. Perry: "In 1961, why didn't you just go ahead and let Mr. Simms bankrupt the corporation? Why did you just get out?"

Keith: "Well, I felt that—to be perfectly frank, I thought Mr. Simms no longer wanted me in the business and that he wanted someone else in, and I didn't think that as long as I was there that it was going to work."

◆   ◆   ◆

Oh, dear love, what turmoil I have brought to us and our heirs. If only I had allowed myself to interpret the signs, we might have escaped all the discord. I know now, and I probably knew then, that you agreed to come to West Virginia in 1949 because of my yearning for the hills and the family. Of course, the frigid temperature, the high mountains of snow and the expanses of ice did nothing to change my emotions. I convinced myself that you were as ready to leave Illinois as I was; but now, fifty-two years later, I shall allow the doubts to drip through the barriers. Neither one of us can be certain of what our lives would have been if we had chosen to stay in Illinois. Perhaps, life would have been more tranquil, but, as the basic elements (you and I) would have remained, our lives together as one would have become similar to what we have created, regardless of where we planted ourselves. The Lord has greatly blessed us and for that I give thanks. Life without you would have been no life at all. We are different in many ways; however, our individual traits, characteristics, beliefs and attitudes complement and mix to produce the people we are today. Often you speak of your love for me and for West Virginia. You have proclaimed us both as your own. God has truly answered us out of the goodness of his love, and has shown us mercy. O, how glorious is our Lord.

◆   ◆   ◆

Mr. Perry continued with the cross-examination of Keith. He inquired if money was ever offered to Keith at any time. Keith responded, "Money was mentioned, but not an amount. The questions asked were like 'How much money would you consider?' or 'How much money would it take?' or 'Would you consider letting me set up trust funds for the children?' The conversation never reached a point as detailed as amount." At last Keith's deposition was at its end.

And further this deponent saith not.

6

The Deposition of Dudley L. Simms, Jr. (Daddy)

Michael Perry examined Daddy for his deposition. It also happened on March 10, 1971. The preliminary questions were as usual: name, address, length of time he had lived in Charleston (Sixty-one years), his age (Sixty-two), marital status, number of children (4), names and where they lived (Patricia Marie Harrison, Huntington; Betty Lee Sears, Charleston; Dudley L. Simms, III, Huntington; John L. Simms, Winston-Salem, North Carolina), Daddy's occupation (merchant).

Mr. Perry: "What type of merchant?"
Daddy: "Retail fabrics."
Mr. Perry: "How long have you been in that business?"
Daddy: "Almost thirty-six years. Over thirty-five years."
Mr. Perry: "Where did you start?"
Daddy: "Charleston, West Virginia."
Mr.Perry: "And roughly, when did you start in Charleston?"
Daddy: "In April of 1935."
Mr. Perry: "And what was the name of the store?"
Daddy: "The Piece Goods Shop."
Mr. Perry: "Now, you are a party plaintiff, one of the people bringing this suit, in a lawsuit that has been commenced in this County in the Circuit Court on behalf of yourself and others against Keith Harrison, are you not?"
Daddy: "Right."

Mr. Perry: "What is the relationship between the plaintiffs in this case?"

Daddy: "Well, Keith is my son-in-law."

Mr. Perry: "And the other plaintiffs are your sons?"

Daddy: "My sons, yes."

Mr. Perry: "What is the purpose and object of that suit? Roughly, why was it brought?"

Daddy: "Well, it was brought because we are organizing our company and there were certain things that hadn't been cleared up in the operation of the company, and we were just trying to clear the air, I guess."

Mr. Perry: "Is it agreeable that when we refer in this deposition to the company that we are referring to The Piece Goods Shop, Inc.?"

Daddy: "Yes."

Mr. Perry: "When did you first meet Mr. Harrison?"

Daddy: "Let's see. How long have you been married, Keith?"

Keith: "Well, we have been married since 1946."

Daddy: "Well, I suppose I met him in 1944 or 1945. In 1944, probably."

The examination continued with questions about how Daddy met Keith (through Keith's uncle, Robert Harrison), how Keith's uncle and Daddy were acquainted. (They were both merchants in Charleston.) Then the questions were directed toward the development of the relationship between Keith and me. The answers included Keith's visiting our home at 401 Fairview Drive, our marriage in 1946, Daddy meeting Keith's parents, including when and where. Mr. Perry also inquired about where Keith and I lived after our wedding.

◆　　◆　　◆

Returning from our honeymoon in Sea Island, Georgia, Keith and I lived on Washington Street, in Charleston, not far from the Capitol

Building. We were both attending Morris-Harvey College. Our apartment was small but comfortable. Housing was scarce due to the end of World War II. Men were returning from the services, and no new houses or apartments had been built. We were forced to pay a one hundred-dollar "reward" to obtain the apartment. We had a bedroom and bath upstairs and a small kitchen and living room downstairs. In the living room, we had two chairs, covered in red flannel chosen from the stock at the Charleston PGS and a round table which had been a play table for my brothers. We cut several inches off the legs and painted it white. We also had a piano that Mother and Daddy previously kept in the recreation room. Keith and I remained in that apartment until June 1947. By then Keith and I were expecting Tia. The summer of 1947 was spent in Freeport, Illinois. Keith's parents were going to Canada for a month, so Keith worked in the stores and we stayed in their home. On their return, Keith and I rode the train back to Charleston and Morris Harvey. Keith attended school and worked as a shoe clerk. We had moved out of the apartment and into a cottage behind my grandmother's (my mother's mother) house on Grant Street. Of course, this pleased me; I loved Grandmother, and she thought I was perfect. Also, she was a wonderful cook. While I was growing up, I often stayed with her. At one time, Grandmother owned a boarding house near the Charleston PGS. I was able to sleep at Grandmother's, walk to the shop to help Daddy or to the library (one of my favorite past times) or to one of the downtown movies or to one of the stores, especially The Diamond Department Store on the corner of Capitol and Washington Streets. These were activities I truly enjoyed.

In the deposition, Mr. Perry asked Daddy how long we lived in Charleston after we were married. He answered, "Approximately a year." Then Mr. Perry questioned where we went after that. Daddy responded, "Freeport, Illinois." Daddy probably forgot, but we really went to Carthage, Illinois. There was a small Lutheran college there that Keith wanted to attend; thus we moved from Charleston to

Carthage. By this period, Tia had been born and was almost four months old. Tia was a beautiful baby. She had dark hair and large blue eyes, surrounded by two-inch eyelashes. In addition, she slept on schedule; she ate on schedule; she even smiled on schedule. And, she had an entire city of admirers. Mother, Keith and Grandmother fussed over who was to take care of her. Obviously, leaving for Carthage was a sad occasion for many of her fans.

Keith and I drove Mother and Daddy's station wagon (with wood panels) to Carthage in January 1948. It was a bitter cold winter. When we arrived, it was late at night. We had rented an upstairs apartment in a house owned by the dean of men. The dean and his family lived downstairs. Exhausted and freezing, we ran upstairs, unlocked the door and jumped into bed, with our clothes still on. I managed to throw my fur coat (a sheared beaver which my parents had given me when I graduated from Stonewall Jackson High School) over the two of us. As I fell asleep, I thought, "I never expected to be using this coat as a blanket, but now I have discovered another use for it. Life is strange, but good."

About five days later, Mother and Daddy brought Tia on a train to St. Louis and then continued by taxi to Carthage, as they had missed their connection in St. Louis. Mother was extremely unhappy. There was not a hotel in Carthage, Illinois, so they stayed in Keokuk, Iowa, across the Mississippi River. Keith's parents drove down from Freeport to visit and to return to Freeport with Mother and Daddy. I knew Mother wanted us to allow Tia to live with them in Charleston, but there was no possible way for that to happen. Also, Mother believed we were living in a place as desolate and cold as the North Pole and, if Tia were to become ill, there wouldn't be a decent doctor or hospital within miles. Just before our parents left for Freeport, we took movies of them. Mother appears to have cried all night, and she was even crying while we were taking the movies. The proof is in the movies which are still in our possession. Well, you won't be surprised to know we moved to Freeport in the summer of 1948. It seemed the best thing to do at the time.

◆   ◆   ◆

Mr. Perry: "Now what did Keith do in Freeport?"

Daddy: "He worked for his father."

Mr. Perry: "And what did his father do?"

Daddy: "He was a grocery man."

Mr. Perry: "What was Keith's financial condition at this time, to the best of your knowledge?"

Daddy: "Well, I know he wasn't over burdened with money, but I just don't know what his financial condition was."

Mr. Perry: "Had you had occasion prior to their moving out there to give them any financial assistance or help them in any way prior to or at the time of the marriage?"

Daddy: "Before the marriage?"

Mr. Perry: "From the time of their marriage until the time they went to Freeport, Illinois."

Daddy: "Well, we always gave them assistance, and I suppose we gave it to them then."

Mr. Perry: "So he certainly wasn't overly blessed with financial resources?"

Daddy: "No, I think that's right."

Mr. Perry: "Now, did they have any children when they were in Freeport, Illinois?"

Daddy: "Well, they were living there, but our daughter came home and had her first baby. In Charleston, I mean."

Mr. Perry: "And then she returned with the grandchild to Freeport?"

Daddy: "Yes."

Mr. Perry: "In the latter part of 1948 or the early part of 1949, did you try to persuade Mr. Harrison and your daughter to return to West Virginia?"

Daddy: "No, I certainly did not try to persuade them."

Mr. Perry: "Did you make any business propositions to him at that time?"

Daddy: "Yes."

Mr. Perry: "What was the purpose of that business proposition?"

Daddy: "That if he wanted to come to Huntington that he could manage the Huntington Piece Goods Shop with the opportunity of becoming a partner, a 40 percent partner, whenever the profits of the company would enable him to pay for it."

Mr. Perry: "This was clearly spelled out by what means?"

Daddy: "Conversation."

Mr. Perry: "Were these personal conversations?"

Daddy: "That's right."

Mr. Perry: "Over the telephone?"

Daddy: "Probably both telephone and maybe face to face."

Mr. Perry: "The face to face, would that occurred in Freeport?"

Daddy: "Probably. I don't remember. It has been a long time ago."

Mr. Perry: "Was there any correspondence or letters back and forth between you and Mr. Harrison on this?"

Daddy: "Not as I recall, but now, as I say, it is a long time ago. Twenty-three years."

Mr. Perry: "Was there just one conversation, and he said yes?"

Daddy: "Oh, several."

Mr. Perry: "What was the nature."

Daddy: "I don't remember the nature of them except what I told you just a moment ago."

Mr. Perry: "Was that your first proposal?"

Daddy: "As far as I remember, yes."

Mr. Perry: "And you never varied from your initial proposal?"

Daddy: "No. I had no reason to."

Mr. Perry: "Now was there any salary discussed?"

Daddy: "I don't recall, but I imagine there was. But I just don't recall."

Mr. Perry: "Do you deny that there was any intimation that this would be a partnership?"

Mr. Payne: "He said it was to be a partnership."

Daddy: "I told you that."

Mr. Perry: "No, I believe what Mr. Simms said was that there was an opportunity to become a partnership."

Daddy: "That's right. That's exactly right."

Mr. Perry: "I am asking, are you denying it was to be a partnership immediately."

Daddy: "Oh, yes, certainly. Not until the stock was paid for."

Mr. Perry: "Now, is stock generally issued in cash with a partnership?"

Daddy: "This was not a partnership. It was a corporation."

Mr. Perry: "And your discussion was always with a corporation with Mr. Harrison."

Daddy: "Oh, yes. Certainly."

Mr. Perry: "To the best you can recall, when were these conversations? In 1948 or 1949?"

Daddy: "There were some expenditures on the store in '48."

Attempting to determine where these conversations occurred, Mr. Perry inquired if Daddy had visited us in Freeport or if Keith and I had visited the family at "401" during the Christmas season of 1948. Daddy responded he was certain we would have been in Charleston most Christmases. Then Lawyer Perry offered the possibility that many of the conversations occurred around that time. Daddy answered, "I think it could have occurred anytime. No more so then than any other time."

◆   ◆   ◆

Their providing a house for us was the next item on the agenda. Daddy insisted this was a personal decision; they found us a home, but they did not intend this to be a part of the offer. I don't believe the house was intended to be part of the original proposal, but it definitely caused us to be more anxious. While we were waiting to come to West Virginia, Mother and Daddy sent us a large professional photograph of the dwelling. In the front yard was a sign on which Daddy had printed our names. We were very excited about living in a brand new home, especially with our expecting another baby. In addition, after our arrival in West Virginia, I was able to choose and purchase blue wool carpet, a solid cherry bedroom suite for Keith and me, gold moire drapes and swags, a Georgetown Galleries mahogany dining room table, chairs, china cabinet, and Victorian furniture for the living room. Keith and I both felt very fortunate. We now had an attractive brick house and a newly decorated store with our family near enough to offer expert advice. Most anyone would have said we were on the road to success and there was no way for us to lose our way, and they would have been half-correct. We did find success, but not with The Piece Goods Shop.

Our success has not been achieved by monetary gains, as much as it has been by spiritual and human endeavors. We pray that God will continue to lead us and help us to bring his heaven to this earth, for his way is the only true way and the only one that shall endure. There are times though, when we allow our desires to drift to the material, especially when viewing the needs of our children, their spouses, and our grandchildren. Then we remind ourselves that God sent his Son to redeem us under law, that we might receive the full rights of sons and daughters. Because we are his children, God has sent the Spirit of his Son into our hearts…and has made us his heirs (Galatians 4: 4-7). This is the only wealth we truly deserve and need, as the result is a life filled with love, joy, peace, patience, kindness, goodness, faithfulness, gentleness, and self-control (Galatians 5: 22-23).

Following the discussion of our home, Mr. Perry directed his efforts to having Daddy report in detail what he had offered us. Daddy declared, "That is he would come down here, or if he wanted to come down and manage the Huntington store, that he would have the opportunity to become a shareholder, when he could pay for the stock out of the earnings. He wasn't suppose to pay out of his pocket, but out of the earnings that he would get out of the business." Next, Mr. Perry asked questions which, when answered, would demonstrate that Daddy was aware Keith had no funds to invest. His reply was: "I didn't think he could personally, but he had other sources where he could have gotten the money, I suppose." The question is: What other sources? Keith certainly could not ask his father, the man he had just abandoned. Also, I do not recall any of this being discussed. We thought the stock was given to Keith to compensate him for leaving Illinois; this matter was not debated. We did not remember any formal meetings being held or Keith being notified. Confidentially, we had no knowledge of corporate business. We trusted Daddy and his lawyers to do what was necessary in forming the business structure of the Huntington PGS.

◆　　　◆　　　◆

Returning to the opening of the shop on April 29, 1949, Mr. Perry stated, "That would have been after these discussions. That is correct, is it not?" Daddy replied in the affirmation.

Mr. Perry: "Had the corporation been formed at the time you were having these discussions with Mr. Harrison?"

Daddy: "The corporation was not formed until afterward. It was formed in June of 1949, right after the store was opened."

Mr. Perry: "But your testimony is that this is the same corporation that you had in your mind all along in connection with your discussion with Mr. Harrison?"

Daddy: "Oh, yes."

◆   ◆   ◆

By examining Daddy's answers to the next questions, it was obvious that the business transactions or discussions were held in the midst of family gatherings. Daddy's reply to one question was: "I am sure there wasn't any business transactions or discussion unless other things entered into it. I mean, I don't think we ever just sat down in a room like this and battled it out."

Mr. Perry returned to the purchasing of the house where we are still living. I am not certain of the purpose of this line of questioning as some questions had been answered previously. The fact is Daddy was confused about most of the details; however, Mr. Perry was not. Mother and Daddy did buy the house at 1016 West Third Street by giving a down payment of $7,500. The cost was $17,500. The house was placed in Mother and Daddy's name. The couple who owned the house was Mr. and Mrs. Billman. Mrs. Billman was a niece of the builder, Mr. Johnson. The Billmans were never able to live in the house as her husband was transferred from Owens Illinois Glass Plant in Huntington (three blocks from our house) before the house was finished. Mr. Johnson was a descendent of the Johnson family who had owned a farm located in the same area. At one time we had a baby sitter (Mrs. Kromer) who said, as a young girl, she had walked the family's herd of cows from Four Pole Creek, down Johnson's Lane (Third Street West) to the Ohio River so she could water the cows. Mrs. Kromer often helped to care for our children. It pleased me to know she had been a part of this area for a long time. I enjoyed mentally watching her stroll through the fields, keeping watch over her charges. Perhaps, this deed helped to develop her deep sense of responsibility.

The date of the deed was March 10, 1949. The Notary Public signed it on March 10, 1949. The sale was recorded in the Cabell County clerk's office on March 14, 1949. Following this episode, it was established that Mother and Daddy obtained a $10,000 mortgage from The First Mortgage Corporation in Huntington on March 11, 1949. The property was subsequently transferred to Keith and me because of a law in West Virginia which discriminates in taxes against property owners not living in their own property; the taxes were reduced by about half after the transfer. The payments which Keith and I were making each month included the taxes and the insurance. Thus, transferring the property to us resulted in a lower monthly payment. (When we first started making payments, the monthly amount was about sixty dollars.) The deed was executed on December 23, 1949 and recorded on December 28, 1949 (the date of our third anniversary). The papers also showed that there was a $7,000 note, signed by Keith and me, made payable to Daddy. There was a release of this deed of Trust executed on December 31,1956 and recorded in Release Book No. 217 at page 89 in Cabell County. Mr. Perry, at this time, revealed that the release of the deed of trust was dated October 28,1949 and was recorded in the Cabell County Clerk's office in Trust Deed Book #571, at page 165, and it indicated that the indebtedness had been fully paid and satisfied. However, Daddy asserted that he had not received any money, and I am certain he had not, as we very seldom had any extra dollars and during that time, we had added expenses due to living in a new house and having an additional child. Our not yet owning an automobile did help us, but not enough to pay a $10,000.00 note. In fact, I don't believe we even realized the debt had been released until this suit materialized. Daddy probably did not mention it, and neither did we. However, Keith and I had been paying the mortgage payment.

◆   ◆   ◆

Mr. Perry: "Now whose idea was it to incorporate the Piece Goods Shop?"

Daddy: "I assume it was mine."

Mr. Perry: "Well, who handled it? What attorney? Charles Gore? Does that sound right?"

Daddy: "Well, it was in that office. I don't know if it was Mr. Samms or Mr. Gore. I am just presuming. I just don't know."

Understanding that Daddy was not able to answer many of these questions due to the lapse of time, Mr. Perry inquired as to who were the incorporators in connection with this? Daddy said, "Myself, Keith Harrison and my wife." Mr. Perry continued, "Where were the papers signed?" Daddy replied, "I do not recall." Furthermore Daddy was not able to respond to many of the next questions. He did not recall if the meeting had occurred in Lawyer Gore's office or if he personally delivered the corporation papers to the other people. Nevertheless, he was able to remember he was president and he had 59 shares issued to him.

Mr. Perry: "But you did at that time receive a stock certificate from The Piece Goods Shop, Inc. for 59 shares."

Daddy: "Well, I don't know if I received it or not, because it was just—if I wrote it, I received it, you know."

Mr. Perry: "Actually all these papers were just kept in one place, were they not?"

Daddy: "Well, they weren't necessarily kept in one place. They might have been, but I don't know."

Mr. Perry: "You didn't have the books and records in one place and then take the stock certificates and put them in another safety deposit box somewhere, did you?"

Daddy: "No."

Mr. Perry: "They were all together?"

Daddy: "As far as that is concerned, because I was waiting for the time to come when Mr. Harrison would pay off his obligation and then give him the stock."

Mr. Perry: "Now, how much money did you put into the corporate treasury of The Piece Goods Shop, Inc?"

Daddy: "Well, I know I put some in during 1948 when we started to remodel the building on Fourth Avenue. And in 1949 I put in additional money, and the total amounted roughly to $15,700.00."

Mr. Perry: "Did you put this money in at the same time this stock was issued to you?"

Daddy: "The stock was never issued, because it was never paid for. So it was never issued."

Mr. Perry: "I am talking about your stock."

Daddy: "Oh, my stock."

Mr. Perry: "Was your stock issued?"

Daddy: "I would have to look it up and and see. I don't know."

Mr. Perry" "Did you have an incorporation meeting?"

Daddy: "Yes."

Mr. Perry: "Were there minutes taken in that meeting?"

Daddy: "I think so."

Mr. Perry: "Where would those minutes be?"

Daddy: "They would be in our—do you have them? Well, the attorney has them."

Mr. Perry: "That is Mr. Payne in Charleston?"

Daddy: "Yes, sir."

Mr. Perry: "Did you elect the Board of Directors at the time?"

Daddy: "I assume we did."

Hence Mr. Perry asked questions concerning the Board of Directors (Keith, Mother, Daddy) "Was there a meeting of the Board of Directors to elect the officers?" (Yes.) "Who were the officers?" (Daddy, President; Keith, Vice President; and Mother, Secretary and Treasurer) "Were the minutes taken?" (Yes.) "Where were they kept?" (Mr. Payne had them.)

What is confusing is Daddy's vague responses. Daddy was sixty-three years old at this time and was still managing the Charleston PGS and was involved with John and Dudley's enterprises. When asked about a stock registry book or a share registration, he referred to Mr.

Payne. Furthermore, when Mr. Perry inquired as to the issue of the stock, Daddy stated, "I don't know what you mean by issued. I had it in my—you know, I had the book, and I don't know. I considered it my company, and the book laid there for years and years. I didn't see any reason to taking my certificate and getting a safety deposit vault and putting it in there, so I didn't bother." He conceded that the certificates and the other records were in one place and under his control and supervision, but Mr. Payne had had them for about two months, in fact, since the suit had begun.

With further questioning, Daddy revealed the stocks, books and papers had been in the safe at the Charleston PGS since they had been delivered to him in 1949. And, subsequently to this time, other stock had been issued in that company. In March of 1961, 40 shares were issued to Daddy, 40 shares to Dudley III, and 20 shares to John L. Simms. According to Daddy's recollection, no amount of money was put into the corporate treasury. They met and issued the stock, after Daddy had written canceled on Keith's shares and Mother's share. Daddy said he recorded his activity in the corporation book. Mr. Perry questioned why certification made out to Keith needed to be canceled if the certificates were not valid. Mr. Perry also inquired where the certificates which Daddy considered "canceled" were located on the date of the depositions (March 10, 1971). Daddy answered in Lawyer Payne's office in Charleston. As to the corporation meeting formally, minutes taken, where the meetings was held, any attorney preparing the minutes, Daddy answered affirmatively, but then would not be able to relate details. For example, when Daddy was asked where the 1961 corporate meeting was held, Daddy answered, "I don't recall." When Daddy was asked if an attorney prepared the minutes or did he, Daddy replied, "I am sure an attorney prepared it, but I don't remember what attorney." Then Mr. Perry inquired if there had been a formal motion to dissolve the corporation. Again Daddy replied, "I don't recall." Another question asked, "Was the corporation liquidated at that time?" Daddy responded, "I don't recall."

Mr. Perry: "Actually, what happened was that after January or February of 1961, you, in your mind, treated it as one thing, and then went ahead and operated it afterward under a new arrangement of 40–40–20, is that correct?"

Daddy: "Yes."

In essence Daddy said no money was invested, certainly not $150.00 a share, and Mother's one share was canceled by Daddy. Moreover more stocks were issued April 7, 1964 to Daddy, John and Dudley III. Thirty–four shares were issued to Daddy, thirty–three to John and thirty–three to Dudley III. This lead to Mr. Perry asking, "How was this accomplished?" Daddy stated, "I presume by minutes." This forced Mr. Perry to ask Daddy if he relinquished certain stock certificates to the corporation and had them reissued. Again Daddy does not recall. Thus Mr. Perry asked about 40 shares given to Dudley III on March 1961 being reduced to thirty–three. "How was that accomplished? Were the old stock certificates turned back in and reissued?" Another answer of "I do not know" was offered.

Mr. Perry: "All right. Now what about after April 7, 1964? Has any subsequent stock been issued? Let's get this clear. As of April 7, 1964, there were still 100 shares outstanding."

Daddy: "Right."

Mr. Perry: "All you had tried to accomplish was a rearrangement of the proportion of stock ownership among you three?"

Daddy: "Right."

Mr. Perry: "And there were still some shares of stocks that were unissued but had been authorized in the original incorporation?"

Daddy: "That I don't know."

Mr. Huddleston: "It speaks for itself."

Mr. Perry: "Since April of 1964, has there been any additional stock issued or transferred among these parties?"

Daddy: "Yes."

Mr. Perry: "When and under what circumstances?"

Daddy: "Now, maybe the attorneys can tell me if I am correct or not. July 31, 1970."

Mr. Perry: "What was done at that time?"

Daddy: "John has 49 ½, Dudley has 49 ½ and I have one."

Mr. Perry: "All right. Now, was this handled on the corporate books at a formal meeting?"

Daddy: "Yes."

Mr. Perry: "Was this in connection with some buy and sell agreement or option between you and your sons, gifts, or what?"

Mr. Payne: "I do not know that is material to the issue here. This is an intra-family matter, Mr. Perry."

Mr. Perry: "No additional monies flowed into the corporate treasury at that time as a result of any of these transactions?"

Daddy: "No."

The next question alluded to any compensation being paid to the director of the corporation, and none had ever been paid. Then Mr. Perry asked if any officers had received any compensation. Daddy repeated, "None." Following, Mr. Payne interrupted the proceedings declaring that Mr. Perry was attempting to seek an inquiry as to what had occurred in the corporation since 1961 in the manner a minority stockholder might be asking about a company in which he is interested. Therefore, as they took the position that Keith had no stock interest in The Piece Goods Shop, Inc., they considered questions concerning compensation as being not material and not relevant to the case and would prohibit inquires which would seek to develop everything that had happened in the corporation since 1961. As would be expected, Mr. Perry affirmed that the other lawyers in his firm and he did contend that there was "a direct relationship between how the affairs of the corporation were conducted prior to 1961 and how they were conducted after 1961," and that they obviously did contend

Keith to be a stockholder. Thus, he was entitled to know the happenings of the corporation concerning compensation, dividends, bonuses, incentives and everything else.

Now, Mr. Payne said he would instruct Daddy not to testify regarding any events of the corporation which occurred after 1961 and had no relationship to whether or not Keith owned stock in the company. Mr. Perry responded, "Let it be clearly understood that if as a result of you so instructing your client we have to go through this again or have the Court determine that we are entitled to this information, that the cost of such a proceeding would rest with your client." To this Mr. Payne replied, "This may be your intention." At this, Mr. Huddleston (Keith's lawyer) stated he wanted in the record that the defenders were entitled to make inquiry of all of the matters pertaining to those which Mr. Payne (one of the prosecutors) had directed to Keith; for example, whether he had received any notice of stockholders' meetings, whether he had received any dividends, and so forth. Mr. Payne defended his position by declaring all of these issues related directly to issues of stock ownership, whether or not Keith felt he had ownership, and whether he asserted it, whereas certain inquiries from Mr. Perry were far afield. "We don't think it is proper to have this corporation laid out in public records for everyone to see by someone who has not yet been established as a stockholder."

At last an area of investigation was reached which intended to clarify how Daddy had structured the business. When Mr. Perry asked Daddy about formal meetings being held by the stockholders and directors and officers of the PGS, Inc. during 1949 until early 1961, Daddy asked for a clarification of "formal." It was defined as written notices sent out to the various stockholders and parties and directors. After determining the time period as prior to 1961, Daddy once again answered, "I don't recall." The next question was similar, only it referred to the meeting for election of officers. Daddy repeated, "I don't recall." He added, "I don't believe we did, but—." Understanding the problem, Mr. Perry asked Daddy if, even though it was called a

corporation, he operated it more or less as a family business. The term
"family business" was then explained. He operated it as a business that
primarily related to himself and his daughter and her husband and his
wife, and the meetings were held on an informal basis, probably discussing and making decisions over the phone. Daddy replied, "Probably."

Changing the topic to finances and statements, it was determined
that Mr. D.P. Krisher, C.P.A. handled the financial records of the corporation since its incorporation until 1961 and even until 1971. Mr
Krisher had been Daddy's accountant as long as I can remember and
was ours while we had the Huntington store. We mailed the cash register tapes, sales tickets, adding machine tapes, bank deposit slips to him
each day, and he prepared the financial statements. It was determined
that no dividends had been declared before 1961 or after 1961.

Following this, the inquiries referred to Keith. He operated the store
from March 1949 (while he was preparing for the opening) until
March 1961. His responsibilities and duties were managing, some buying, and advertising. Mr. Perry also questioned Daddy's involvement.
He admitted to assisting Keith in the beginning but decreasing his
activity as Keith became more familiar with the business.

Mr. Perry: "Do you recall what his salary was during this period of
time?"

Daddy: "I know what his salary was in 1961 when he left the corporation."

Mr. Perry: "What was it then?"

Daddy: "$800.00 a month."

Mr. Perry: "Do you recall roughly what it was when he first
started?"

Daddy: "No."

Mr. Perry: "What were the circumstances surrounding his leaving
that particular store in 1961?"

Daddy: "Well, the store had been going downhill for some time—years, I guess. And it got so bad that the suppliers started writing me letters that they would not ship us any more goods unless their bills were paid."

Mr. Perry: "Now did you discuss this situation with Mr. Harrison?"

Daddy: "I did."

Mr. Perry: "In what matter?"

Daddy: "The same manner I just told you."

Mr. Perry: "Over the phone, or did you come down?"

Daddy: "Oh, I came down. I imagine both. But I remember very well coming down to Huntington."

Mr. Perry: "What did you request him to do?"

Daddy: "Well, I had done all the requesting I could up to that time. I told him that with things as they were, that the store was going bankrupt, and in fact that I had every intention in the world of putting the store into bankruptcy, and that—well, I am kind of jumping—and I would have put it into bankruptcy, but I have a good friend that is President of our buying office in New York City, and I called him on the phone and he strongly advised me against it. This wasn't right at the same time. It might have been a week later. I don't remember the exact time, but he strongly advised me against it because he thought it would reflect on me personally and upon the other stores that we owned."

Mr. Perry: "How many stores did you own at that time, Mr. Simms?"

Daddy: "In 1961."

Daddy: "We had six stores."

Mr. Perry: "Where were the stores?"

Daddy: "Huntington, West Virginia; Charleston, West Virginia; Parkersburg, West Virginia; Beckley, West Virginia; Bluefield, West Virginia; and Marietta, Ohio. Now, these were under different corporations."

Mr. Perry: "Every one of them?"

Daddy: "No, the Parkersburg and Marietta store was under the name of The Piece Good Shop, Incorporated of Parkersburg."

Mr. Perry: "Did you own stock in that one?"

Daddy: "Yes. The Beckley and the Bluefield Store was under the name of The Piece Goods Shop, Incorporated of Beckley, West Virginia. Charleston was then and always has been an individual ownership."

Daddy owned forty shares in the Parkersburg Corporation, James Butner (husband of Mother's sister Georgia) owned forty, and Otto Becker (President of the Buying and Research Syndicate) owned 20. In the Beckley Corporation Daddy owned 40, Roland Hinckley (a long time friend of Daddy's and manager of the Beckley Corporation) owned 40, and Otto Becker 20. After presenting this information, Daddy returned to conditions at the Huntington Shop. "I came to Huntington after pleading with Keith and our daughter about the way conditions were and how bad—this went on for years, and I came down to bring it to a head and I told them that the store was going to be put in bankruptcy, and I thought he hadn't done the job, or words to that effect, and that he ought to resign. And I gave him, I believe, a check for $800.00 for severance pay, and he brought up the idea of stock, which he never—."

At the mention of stock, Mr. Perry became extremely interested. He asked Daddy, "How was the idea of stock discussed specifically?" Daddy replied, "It was discussed that the stock was no concern at all, because it was never issued and he never paid for it." Daddy continued that, as he remembered, Keith made no objection. He gave Daddy the keys to the store and left, and there was nothing disagreeable about the situation at all. Neither Keith nor Daddy created a disturbance.

What Daddy said about Keith's and his leaving the store without a disturbance was true. I was also present as we had inventoried the merchandise and cleaned the shop. I had become more active in the shop after the birth of three more children: Scott in 1955, Sean in 1956, and

Dirk in 1957. It was difficult to support a family of seven on $800.00 a month, so Keith attempted to supplement our income with other jobs and I assisted at the shop. I am not saying this is why the business was failing; however, we attempted to adjust. The financial results were not positive. In addition, Daddy was not receptive to ideas such as opening another store, possibly in Ashland or Portsmouth, or our wholesaling notions to the other shops; ideas which were later used in the corporation. Looking back, it is my opinion that Daddy had lost all faith in us, and the shop under our management. Also, John and Dudley were now twenty–four and ready to become more active in the business. Besides, Keith and I truly thought the Huntington store would close when we left the operation. Even the Anderson—Newcomb Department Store on Third Avenue had closed the yard goods department which had been the owners' favorite area.

My parents had a black and white print in the recreation room, which reminded me so much of Keith and me. The picture depicted an old black man walking through the snow, carrying a jug of whiskey, which had a hole in it large enough to allow the whiskey to filter out and fall behind him as he walked. Under the picture were the words: "Ignorance is Bliss." We truly were ignorant. But, at the same time, we had a rich and rewarding life. Though we were not happy to leave the store, we felt, with God's help, we would survive. We had discussed the shares and decided not to ask for any monetary reimbursement as we were led to believe all that remained was the inventory, which would be sent to the other stores. Keith had not attended any meetings or discussions; no one had spoken to us about the end situation. Keith felt, whether it was worth anything or not, the shares should be left to our children in our will. I know, for most people, it is difficult to believe, but we considered the Huntington PGS a lost cause (something like a country which has lost a war and its currency has no value). As surprised as we were when the Huntington store reopened, we still saw no connection to us. The business was a new and different organization. It was ours no longer.

When Mr. Perry asked Daddy, "You didn't request him to execute any instruments at that time?" Daddy answered, "No, I did not, because I did not think they were necessary." Daddy did not have a formal meeting of the corporation or of the board of directors to decide what was necessary. He made the determination by himself.

The bank we used for the Huntington PGS from 1949 to 1961 was The Guaranty. It was on Ninth Street between Sixth Avenue and Fifth Avenue. The PGS continued to use that bank. Daddy was renamed the President of the Corporation, even though, by this time (1971), he had only one share. Mr. Perry remarked, "That's a powerful one share you have."

Now Daddy offered a reason for the Huntington PGS not going into bankruptcy. Some time later, maybe a week, Daddy called Otto Becker and he advised Daddy against the move. In fact, he offered to invest money in the shop. Ultimately he loaned the Huntington PGS $6,000.00, James Butner loaned $6,000.00, and Roland Hinkley loaned $4,000.00. Mr. Hinkley's and Mr. Butner's loans came from the appropriate corporation. Mr. Becker's loan was individual. Formal notes were executed to secure these loans, and there was no collateral. Then Mr. Perry concluded that, "In the final analysis, it was determined that it was still a profitable enterprises, but the primary concern was the management." In a manner of agreeing, Daddy added, "Well, I thought it could—I always thought it could have been a profitable enterprise, or I wouldn't have opened it, and wouldn't have kept it going."

It was at that point Mr. Perry began questioning Daddy about other businesses which were now in existence and included in the corporation.

Mr. Perry: "What is the relationship between The Piece Goods Shop, Inc. and Simms Realty?"

Mr. Payne: "Do you think that has a bearing on this lawsuit, Mr. Perry?"

Mr. Perry: "Yes."

Mr. Payne: "How so?"

Mr. Perry: "Well, I think we are entitled to know, first, how these business affairs between these corporations are conducted in the sense of whether formal meetings are held, notices, et cetera, and I think it certainly has a tremendous bearing upon the eventual outcome of the lawsuit, and namely, what does 40% of the corporation represent?"

Mr. Payne: "Well, that is something quite apart from the issue of who owns the stock of this company, and I think you are getting too far afield."

Mr. Perry: "Are you instructing your client not to answer?"

Mr. Payne: "I am."

Mr. Perry: "I am asking him similar questions with regard to Simms Franchise, Fabric Investment, Consolidated Fabrics, PGS Corporation, and Associated Fabric Corporation. Are you instructing your client not to answer?"

Mr. Payne: "I am instructing my client not to answer."

Mr. Perry: "How many Piece Goods Shops does this company in the lawsuit operate?"

Mr. Payne: "Do not answer that."

Mr. Perry: "In connection with your contention that Mr. Harrison does not own any stock in the company, when and where were you first notified or advised of any contention on his part to the contrary?"

Daddy: "I don't believe Mr. Harrison ever mentioned it?"

Mr. Perry: "Well, are you not bringing a lawsuit in which you specifically allege that Mr. Harrison claims or contends to own stock in The Piece Goods Shops?"

Daddy: "Yes."

Mr. Perry: "What precipitated that lawsuit?"

Daddy: "Well, we were making certain changes and we were trying to clear the books and we were advised to have Mr. Harrison sign—I suppose it was a release. I didn't read it, and I don't know, but I suppose it was a release. I don't know what was in it. I never saw the——."

Mr. Perry: "But this was a conclusion that you and your attorneys or someone reached, and not something Mr. Harrison said?"

Daddy: "No, Mr. Harrison has never mentioned stock to me in twenty years."

Mr. Perry: "What action has been taken, to the best of your knowledge, to secure such an assignment or release of any stock owned by Mr. Harrison?"

Finally, Daddy admitted my brother Dudley asked Keith to sign the release; however, he insisted he had nothing to do with the preparation or the request. He knew the papers for the release were prepared in Mr. Payne's office in December 1970, and he was aware of Dudley's conversations with the attorneys and their advice concerning Keith's releasing the stock.

Requesting the release of the stock was not the only action taken. The corporation had opened a business (retail and wholesale) on route 60 and continued to operate a retail shop in downtown Huntington. Tia, some of our sons, and myself worked in these businesses. Dudley was managing these stores at the time of the request, and he informed us our services were no longer needed. As I was teaching at Huntington High School, this action did not greatly influence our income, but Tia had only been married a little over a year and her husband was attending Marshall University. Another retaliation was the closing of charge accounts in Huntington which belonged to Mother and Daddy, and which I was permitted to use. And, Mother and Daddy were helping us to send Sean (our third son) to Greenbrier Military Institute. Sean returned home to public school.

Continuing Daddy's deposition, Mr. Perry inquired, "Have you ever discussed this lawsuit personally with Mr. Harrison?"

Daddy: "No."

Mr. Perry: "Have you ever discussed it with your daughter?"

Daddy: "No, sir. I had a conversation with her after Dudley's conversation with Mr. Harrison over the phone one time. But that was before the lawsuit."

Mr. Perry: "What was the nature of the conversation?"

Daddy: "Well, I just wanted to—as well as I remember, I asked her why or how could they do such a thing after as nice as I had been to them. That's just about it."

Mr. Perry: "And that is the only conversation?"

Daddy: "And that he didn't own the stock, and I didn't see any—regardless of what anybody said or what a judge said, that I knew and I thought that he knew that they didn't own the stock."

Mr. Perry: "That was before the lawsuit?"

Daddy: "Yes."

Mr. Perry: "And that is the only conversation you had?"

Daddy: "That is the only one with either one. I haven't seen Mr. Harrison until today, and that is the only conversation I have had with our daughter."

This was the only attempt Daddy made to settle the situation without a lawsuit; nonetheless, the suit had been filed and we had received the papers. In fact, when Dudley came to our home, Keith told him to allow conditions to stay as they were before the suit. We did not plan to ask for power or money. The shares were to be a symbol of our involvement in the Huntington PGS. We could not understand why it was so important that we give Daddy, Dudley, and John worthless stock, and they did not explain.

Mother called me and my sister Betty Lee Sears wrote me. These contacts were disturbing; but, as neither Betty Lee nor Mother were anymore knowledgeable than I was, I did not pursue the situation. Betty Lee was now in the midst of a divorce and dependent on the business, as was Mother. Understanding their attitudes was not difficult.

As Mr. Perry had completed his examination of Daddy, Mr. Payne asked Daddy if he had told Keith anything during the 1948–1949 period that would have given him the impression he had received the stock as a gift. Daddy answered, "No." Next, Mr. Payne referred to the PGS Inc. of Parkersburg and the PGS Inc. of Beckley. He asked Daddy if the managers (Mr. Hinckley and Mr. Butner) had purchased their shares, and Daddy replied, "They purchased them."

The last questions of Mr. Payne's cross-examination dealt with our coming to Huntington from Freeport, Illinois.

Mr. Payne: "Now going back to the time again in 1948 and 1949 when you were discussing with Mr. Harrison his coming to manage the Huntington store which was to be organized, was Mr. Harrison anxious or reluctant to come to Huntington?"

Daddy: "Well, I had most of the conversation with our daughter."

Mr. Payne: "What was her attitude."

Daddy: "She was very anxious to get back to West Virginia. She didn't think her husband was making a salary that they could live on, so we often sent her money to come home and go back, and I think she was very happy with the opportunity to come to Huntington."

Mr. Payne: "That is all we have."

And further this deponent saith not.

7

Illustrations

Mary Springman Best
with great-grandson Keith

At Ward-Belmont College in Nashville,
Fall 1945
Left to right
Front: Dudley III, Betty Lee, Patty
Back: John, Mother, Daddy

Keith Harrison 1946

Patricia Simms and Keith Harrison
Freeport, Illinois
February 1946
After Keith returned from the South Pacific

Belvidere Park on th shores of Lake Geneva, Wisconsin
Vacation spot of the Harrison and Simms families
1945 and 1946

Patty and Keith at the pavilion in Lake Geneva, Wisconsin
Summer 1946

Our wedding reception at the Daniel Boone Hotel in Charleston, West
Virginia, December 28, 1946
Left to right: Jack Krantz, Mary Gail Kelly, Jack Harrison (Keith's
brother), Margie Berry, Glenn Harrison (Keith's father), Keith, Patty,
Daddy, David Berry, Betty (my sister), William Pittman (my cousin),
Martha Farrell, Roberta Harrison (Keith's cousin),
Bonnie Lee Butner (my cousin and flower girl).

Our wedding reception, in the ballroom of the Daniel Boone Hotel,
December 28, 1946
Left to Right: Glenn G. and Berneice Harrison (Keith's parents)
Keith and Patty
Opal and Dudley Simms Jr. (my parents)

Wedding Reception 1946
Left to right: Otto Becker (President of Buying and Research Syndicate in
New York) my Uncle Kenneth Andrews, behind him is my uncle Jim Butner
Walter Durkin (sold Strauss laces to the Piece Goods Shop), my
grandmother's second husband Albert Ellison, Keith's Uncle Bob—who
introduced Keith and me (the brother of Keith's father), and last, my
maternal grandfather John Riddle (my grandmother's first husband)

Wedding Reception 1946
Left to Right: Keith's Uncle Bob's wife Clara Harrison,
Keith's great-aunt Margaret Hayes (his Grandmother Harrison's sister),
Keith's grandmother Ardell Harrison, and last, my maternal grandmother
Laura Mae Riddle Ellison

Patty and Tia Harrison
January 1948

Tia Marie Harrison
Grandmama and Granddaddy's home in Charleston, West Virginia
Christmas 1948

Left to right: Mother's sisters Stachia Andrews and Georgia Butner, my maternal grandmother Laura Mae Riddle (1st husband) Ellison (2nd husband), Opal Simms (my mother) spring of 1948

Home of Patty and Keith Harrison
1016 Third Street West Huntington, West Virginia
Fall 2000

The Simms family and descendants 1957 at 401 Fairview Drive,
Charleston, WV
(Left to right)
Back row: John Simms, Keith Harrison, Dudley Simms, Jack
Sears, Dudley Simms III

Seated on sofa: Patricia Harrison holding son Sean Harrison, Tia Harrison,
Opal Simms holding Grandson Dirk Harrison, Betty Sears holding
daughter Tracy Sears and son John Sears

Seated in front: Keith Harrison Jr. (Karry) and Scott Harrison

Dudley Lee Simms Jr. in the White House with
President of the United States, Dwight D. Eisenhower
October 1958

Mother and Daddy's 50th Anniversary
December 29, 1975
Front Row: Betty, Mother, Daddy, Patty
Back Row: Dudley, Barbara, Keith, Victoria, John

Christmas 1979 at "401"
Daddy is on the front walk

Mother and Daddy
Christmas 1981 at "401"

Daddy, Christmas 1981 at "401"

Patricia at a party given by her family after commencement exercises
May 1983

The children of Opal and Dudley Simms Jr., at a brunch in Winston-Salem, North Carolina, given for Tracy Simms (Dudley's daughter) who was marrying Robert Winston III
May 16, 1987
Left to right: John Lee Simms, Betty Lee Sears, Patricia Harrison, Dudley Lee Simms III

Patty, Keith and Family, 50th Anniversary, December 28, 1996,
Greenbrier Resort

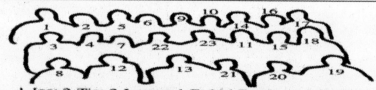

1-Joe; 2-Tia; 3-Laura; 4-Bobbi Daulton; 5-Robert
(Sean); 6-Laura; 7-Laine; 8-Robert (Beau)
Harrison; 9-Keith (Karry); 10-Linda; 11-Ashleigh;
12-Karry (Chase); 13-Keith III (Blake) Harrison;
14-Scott; 15-Lindsay Harrison; 16-Mary Jo;
17-Dirk; 18-John (Cory); 19-Chad; 20-Chanse;
21-Clark Harrison; 22-Patricia; 23-Keith Harrison

Keith Harrison with first great-grandchild,
Travis Menke, Jr.
Christmas Day 2001

PART IV

o o o o o o o o o o o o o o o o o o o o o o o o o o o o o o

Soon spreads the dismal shade
Of Mystery over his head;
And the caterpillar and fly
Feed on the Mystery

—Verse 4
"The Human Abstract"
by
William Blake, 1794

8

Settlement

There would have been no settlement if Keith were permitted to retain the stocks that Daddy, Dudley III and John contended were canceled. However, Keith was sued and, as Keith and I personally had no funds to pay a law firm to defend him, we were forced to find a firm that would accept our case on a contingency basis. We were fortunate to obtain the law firm of Huddleston, Bolen, Beatty, Porter, and Copen. If we had remained silent, the shares would have fallen to Daddy, Dudley III, and John by default, which to us would have been equal to saying we never truly believed Keith was an owner in the corporation. We strongly believed he was. Keith and I both prayed for guidance and spoke with our pastor, family and friends.

Huddleston Letters

Our law firm and their law firm actually acted as our spokesmen. Several letters were exchanged as the two firms negotiated the settlement. A letter from each firm remains in our possesion. On May 26, 1971, Mr. Huddleston wrote to Mr. Payne that the testimonies of Daddy and of Keith had been carefully studied in conjunction with the record evidence which had been furnished to them including: (1) the Certificate of Incorporation; (2) the minutes of the organization meetings of the stockholders and directors and the by-laws adopted and approved at such meetings; (3) all subsequent minutes of stockholder and directors meetings, with the exception of annual and special meetings of the board of directors held on April 15, 1968 and August 15, 1968, respectively, and meetings held on September 19, 1969, which were not furnished to our lawyers; (4) the three stock certificate stubs and the three unsigned stock certificates for 59, 40 and 1 share respectively, issued in the names of Dudley L. Simms, Keith G. Harrison and Opal M. Simms, dated June 26, 1949 (the same date of the organization meeting); (5) the opening ledger and journal entries of the corporation which showed $15,000.00 paid in capital and that $15,000.00 of capital stock of the par value of $150.00 was issued; (6) the balance sheets of the corporation for July 31, 1960 and December 31, 1960 (Keith and I left the shop in February of 1961.), each of which shows that $15,000.00 was paid as capital for common stock, as do the July 31, 1966, 1967, 1968, 1969, and 1970 balance sheets; (7) the 1949 and 1950 U.S. corporate income tax returns which were required by law to be signed by two corporate officers and which stated they were prepared by Donald P. Krishner (Daddy's accountant who had the care of the corporation's books) and specifically said that Keith G. Harrison owned 40% of the common stock of the corporation.

Following this, Mr. Huddleston stated in the letter, "It is our opinion from such analysis that the record evidence conclusively supports Mr. Harrison's testimony and completely refutes that of Mr. Simms, even if we assume Mr. Simms' testimony that Mr. Harrison never became a stockholder would be admissible." However, Mr. Huddleston did declare that they considered such testimony as not admissible because the organization minutes were signed which showed that both Daddy and Keith were present at the meeting and in the minutes it stated that each agreed to sign the minutes "in evidence of that fact and in evidence of their agreement to the accuracy and sufficiency of these minutes." These minutes were signed at the end by Daddy and Keith. In the minutes there appeared the following "...and that they and each of them will sign said by-laws as stockholders after said stock has been issued to them by this Corporation." Therefore it was agreed by the organizers that the by–laws were only to be signed by each as a stockholder and after stock had been paid for and issued to an organization by the corporation. The last page of the by–laws revealed that Daddy and Keith signed the by-laws in two separate places, first as organizers and second as <u>stockholders</u> and directors of the corporation. As the minutes and the by-laws were signed by each as stockholders of the corporation (Article XI; subparagraphs (c) to (f), inclusive), Daddy was bound by his agreement with Keith that his stock had been paid for and issued and that Keith was a stockholder of the corporation. The fact that Daddy neglected to have any of the stock certificates signed was not important as Daddy claimed that he and Mother were stockholders of the corporation even though their certificates had not been signed by officers of the corporation.

Next Mr. Huddleston declared that to say Keith, as a stockholder, had waived his right or was estrained from asserting his ownership of stock in the corporation because of the concerted action of Daddy and my brothers (who did not pay any monies to the corporation or to Keith for the stock issued to them) did not require any further comment. If Daddy and my brothers should have attempted to introduced any evidence to the effect that they had been prejudiced (as was suggested in a letter dated March 30,1971 from Mr. Payne), Keith was entitled to introduce evidence which (in the opinion of Mr. Huddleston and the other partners) would establish that Keith was the one who had been prejudiced due to the large and unreasonable amounts they had withdrawn from the corporation since 1961. Keith's lawyers concluded that Daddy, Dudley and John had been more than amply rewarded for any energies they might have expended in increasing the value of the corporate assets, and that they believed that this could have been established beyond question.

In addition, an analysis had been made of the financial information furnished to Mr. Huddleston and to his partners in a letter written by Charles Stacy dated April 9, 1971. They considered the various factors stated in that letter (excluding "restrictions on transfer," as they were not aware of any). They also declared invalid the by–law provision which gave an owner of a majority of the corporation stock the option to purchase minority interests at book value because of the provisions of the Stock Transfer Act which was in effect in West Virginia at the time this provision was adopted. Taking into consideration the relevant factors and in light of all the competent evidence, Huddleston and the other lawyers deemed the amount of $10,000.00 offered as settlement, in Mr. Payne's letter of March 30, 1971, a pittance and so it was declined.

In response to this offer, Mr. Huddleston and firm valued what they considered to be Keith's 40% interest in a corporation such as the Piece Goods Shop, Inc., and claimed it had a minimum value of between approximately $140,000.00 and $185,000.00. This did not include any allegations in Keith's counterclaim, which in their opinion had substance in view of the advised amount the individual plaintiffs had withdrawn from the corporation as salaries. However, Mr. Huddleston had been authorized by Keith to accept a cash payment equivalent to the book value of a 40% interest in the corporation at the time of settlement but, in any event, not less than $91,839.60, the book value of such an interest in the corporation as of July 31, 1970. This letter was mailed to William C. Payne and Spilman, Thomas, Battle and Klostemeyer.

Payne's Response

The response to this letter was dated May 28, 1971. At the beginning of the letter Mr. Payne commented on various items in Mr. Huddleston's letter of May 26, 1971. The first comment alluded to the 1949 and 1950 tax returns, which Mr. Payne and his office believed were signed by Keith alone. They knew of no requirement that officers sign the return. Of course, the point was that Mr. Krisher (Daddy's accountant) had prepared the tax returns in which it was stated Keith was 40% owner of the common stock.

Secondly, Mr. Payne said they (the lawyers in his office) thought the language from the organization minutes, which Mr. Huddleston had quoted in his letter, had much probative force. Mr. Payne did not think the organization papers were an accurate reflection of the actual circumstances; he believed the capital had been paid into the corporation before the organization meetings, and the stock certificates were in fact never issued. (My question to this is why were they recorded into the ledger and journal as issued?)

The third comment stated, "We do not agree with your conclusion that the stock purchase right contained in the by–laws is invalid and can perceive no basis for such an argument." (As I personally have not been formally educated in the legality of laws and information, I may be incorrect; but, as I read Mr. Huddleston's letter, the by–law provision was considered invalid because the state of West Virginia's Stock Transfer Act remained in effect at this time and state law supercedes the by-laws of the corporation.)

Next, Mr. Payne offered the use of the defense of laches. (The word laches is defined as a delay in asserting a right or a claim.) He cited the case of *Snyder V. Charleston and Southside Bridge Company*, 65 W. Va. (1909). The Court said, "The plaintiff delayed for six years to take any active steps for the enforcement of his right, knowing for at least five years of that time, that he was not recognized by said company as one of its stockholders." Though the Supreme Court had found Snyder to be a stockholder, the court dismissed the case. (Does anyone but Mr. Payne and the others in his firm consider this a valid comparison? Keith did not take active steps for the enforcement of his right; he was forced into taking a position he truly did not choose to pursue. His desire was to remain owner of 40% of a defunct corporation. It was a symbol of his activities from 1949 until 1961. We could not understand why anyone else would want the shares. Of course, we later became aware of Daddy's and Dudley's and John's immediate need of the shares.

Mr. Payne cited two more cases relating to laches. Then he repeated what he had written in a previous letter on March 30. In that letter, he and his office reviewed some of the evidence showing that Keith knew or should have known he had a claim in 1961 at the latest. Quoting part of the letter of March 30, 1971, "Even if Harrison was originally entitled to stock, at this late date he is certainly in no position to secure an adjudication that he is in fact an owner of stock in this company. He claims he believed from 1949 on he owned 40 shares. Now 21 years later, he asserts ownership and asks for a certificate." (Did he ask for a certificate?)

"At least from 1961 on he knew or should have known the plaintiffs did not recognize his alleged stock ownership. At that time when Harrison left the company, in 1961, he knew that Dudley Simms, Sr. felt that Harrison had no stock interest because Mr. Simms told him that the stock had not been paid for and was never issued. Harrison must have understood the importance of this because he told Dudley Simms, III in December of 1970 that he, Harrison, wondered why he wasn't asked to 'sign out' of the company in the same manner that he 'signed in'."

The next section of the March 30 letter dealt with Keith's telling Dudley III in December of 1970 he feared his statute of limitations or some time period had run out on his claim to the stock. Also the letter referred to Keith's saying in his deposition that in the period of almost 10 years since 1961 there had been no indication of any kind that the plaintiffs regarded him as owner of the stock. According to Mr. Payne "a prudent owner of 40 shares of stock in this company would certainly begin to wonder whether his claim to ownership was recognized."

Next Mr. Payne reiterated what had been said by our lawyers about Keith's not receiving notice of stockholders' meetings.. Of course, Mr. Payne wanted everyone to know that the pre–1961 situation was different because Keith was in management and privy to all the major corporate decisions. (I wouldn't go as far as to say "all"; in fact, I would probably say "few, if any.")

Another comment related to Keith's waiting with his claim and failing to inquire about the true status of his stock while the value of the company was increasing far beyond its value in 1961. Now Mr. Payne mentions Dudley's and John's entrance into the business with no knowledge of the events of 1949. They assumed that they and Daddy alone owned the company. (We thought a new corporation had been formed.) Just to make Keith's actions appear more deviant, it is noted the July 31,1970 balance sheet for this company shows the net worth to be $229,599.00 and, in 1961, the company was insolvent. (I wonder what businesses were included on the balance sheet.)

As a last resort, Mr. Payne, declares, "I can't believe that under these circumstances a court of equity will give aid to Harrison." He then reminded the readers of the letters that the records of the company showed in early 1961 store receipts "resumably coming into the hands of Mr. Harrison" were never deposited in the company bank accountant; however, these amounts were written off by the company. (Of course, Mr. Payne would have known nothing of this, but we brought those deposits home to be made the next day. I placed them in the top of my closet. When I returned to the closet the next morning, the deposit bags were empty. We assumed the woman we had employed to assist us at home had taken the money. We never pursued the affair. She stopped working for us and moved out of the state; later she even asked us for recommendations. We never answered the letters.)

Of course, one of the last paragraphs in Mr. Payne's letter of May 28, 1971 won the prize for attempting to intimidate the opposition. He asserted, "We think we can prevail. In addition to our superior positions on the law and evidence, the 'equities' seem to be with us. The Court may well view Mr. Harrison as a man who has contributed nothing to the success of the company and who wishes to profit by the success of others who worked without the slightest hint or knowledge of his claim to ownership. Nonetheless, we would certainly not attempt to persuade you that there are no substantial arguments available on your side of the case. And we have not advised our clients that winning is 100% certain. More importantly, our clients are willing to accept a fair settlement so as to keep this family affair out of the courts and thereby avoid the bitterness which can result from court contests. But we have been instructed that if a fair settlement figure cannot be agreed upon, we should promptly proceed to trial and have these matters resolved in that manner."

At this point, Keith's offer to settle for the amount of $91,839.60 was declined. However, a counter offer of $40,000.00 was presented asserting any settlement would entail releases of all claims between all parties, dismissal of the law suit, and counterclaims with prejudice and relinquishment by Mr. Harrison of any claim to stock in The Piece Goods Shop, Inc.

As expected, the counter action was declined; thus, a request for a meeting between attorneys to resolve the case was suggested during the week of June 1. The meeting was held, and Daddy, Dudley and John finally accepted Keith's offer of $91,839.60. Our law firm received one third of the settlement. Most people would say we had won the suit; I know the Simms family felt they had lost; but, in all honesty, we felt that we personally had lost. We truly wanted the stock, even if it had no monetary value. The problem was Daddy had not closed the corporation correctly; it was revealed that Keith's 40% pertained to the entire corporation and my brothers needed absolute ownership to place the business on the market, an action that had to occur immediately as my brothers were having problems with funds. Thus, the reason became evident for their not reorganizing the company and allowing us to retain the shares, which would have become momentarily worthless.

After the settlement The Piece Goods Shop, Inc. became part of the stock market, and we invested $70,000.00 into CD'S for a period of time. Little by little we did spend the money. We bought a brand new Buick and paid cash for it. In 1974, I went to the University of Kentucky and earned a Specialist's Degree in Foreign Language Education. During this year, I took a year leave of absence from teaching at Huntington High School. I attended classes in Lexington through the week and returned home on the weekends. In addition, one summer Keith and I visited Europe, rented a car and drove through the Netherlands, Germany, Austria and Switzerland. We remained at a town as long as we wanted and then called ahead for reservation when we were ready to leave. We returned home during the time of Nixon's resignation. And, in 1977, we used a CD to secure Karry's loan to open Heritage Station Restaurant, which Karry later repaid to us. Surely all of these activities enriched our lives, but if we had not received the settlement, we believe we would have been able to exist without it. Oh, yes, we finally remodeled our kitchen; we even bought an electric dishwasher. Of course, by this time our children were grown and living elsewhere in Huntington. While our children lived at home, they took turns doing the dishes each evening; if we had owned an automatic dishwasher they would have missed the enlightening and bonding experience of cleaning the kitchen with one of their siblings.

Now do not expect this to end my story, for it does not. Like the caterpillar and the fly in verse four of Blake's poem "The Human Abstract," we now fed upon the mystery, the deceit of the entire episode, which allowed us to continue life without knowing exactly what had happened in the past and surmising what might possibly happen in the future.

9

Relationships

Approximately three years later, my parents called and invited us to meet them at church (The Baptist Temple on Quarrier Street in Charleston). We were elated to be asked. We met them, attended church and then visited at 401 Fairview Drive. On that day nothing was mentioned concerning the suit. Later my mother asked me several times to explain our viewpoint, but I never did. I knew if I had, the result would be a debate and she would feel she had to support one side over the other. I could not comprehend anything good coming from such actions. Even after their deaths in 1983 (Mother died on February 23, 1983 and Daddy died on March 1, 1983.) we were not able to reunite with Dudley's and John's families except for Mother's and Daddy's fiftieth wedding anniversary in 1975, weddings of our children, and deaths. My sister and I returned to the close relationship we enjoyed before the suit; for this I shall forever give thanks to our Lord. As I said previously, Betty and her husband Jack Sears divorced in 1971 and their children lived with him until they were adults, so her life had changed greatly. Both my sister and my mother had experienced severe problems with alcohol but were able to overcome this disease with God's help and the counseling of the Fellowship Hall in Greensboro, North Carolina; this happened three years after the suit, in the year 1974. I am so proud of them and anyone who has been able to overcome any type of addiction. We personally have dealt with addiction within our own circle of children and have experienced the hell it creates for all, whether it is the person addicted or one of those touched by the effects.

In February 8, 1974, Dudley III and Barbara (Dudley's wife since 1958) and John and Victoria (John's wife since 1967) wrote a letter to Keith and me. It began:

Dear Patty and Keith:

This is just a short note saying that we have been thinking of you and have been remembering you in our prayers.

Also, we have forgiven you for past events and accept the fact that you sincerely thought you were doing what God would have you do in this circumstance.

We wish to ask for your forgiveness also in the manner which we responded to your actions. You are still our sister and brother-in-law. Only God knows the truths hidden in all of our hearts.

We hope that you accept this letter in the spirit in which it was written and do not try to find some ulterior motive which was not meant.

We do not know if things will ever be as they were and are not sure how great the situation was.

We love you both but its hard to overcome our natural sinful feelings. So forgive us again for our shortcomings for now and in the future.

Stop by and see us if you are ever in Winston-Salem.

Sincerely,

Dudley III, Barbara
John, Victoria

This letter was typewritten but signed personally.
On February 28, 1974,Keith and I wrote a letter in reply.

Dear Dudley, John, Victoria and Barbara,

There are no words to describe the joy that your letter brought. Keith says it is the most wonderful Valentine's gift we have ever received. At least, I know it was one that was filled with love, as only love heals all wounds. (Some say time does, but I don't agree.)

As for forgiving, there is nothing to forgive. I don't believe we have the power to judge; therefore we lack the need to forgive, and that in itself is a blessing. We have never blamed any of you for anything. You did what you considered right. That's all there is to it. Our love for all of you has never decreased, only increased. We are a family and nothing will change that, neither time nor words nor actions nor emotions. Love is eternal.

What we should do is praise our Lord who has given us so much, and ask him to bless us and remain with us. This comes not because of acts which please him, but because of our faith and His love. If only we could have such understanding!

As for things being the same, we can never return to life as it were, but who wants to do so. Life increases with richness, as our days grow older.

We both look forward to being with you sometime in the future.

Thank you for caring,

As ever,

Keith,
and
Patty

No other communication comes to mind until the middle of summer in 1975. One Sunday, Keith and I met Barbara and Dudley at Fifth Avenue Baptist Church. It has been our church since the autumn of 1949 and was Barbara's and Dudley's church while they lived in Huntington. We attended the service, had our pictures taken, and we may have had lunch; on September 3, 1975, they wrote us.

Mr. and Mrs. Keith Harrison
1016 West 3rd Street
Huntington, W. Va. 25701

Dear Patty and Keith:

Enclosed are photos from our midsummer visit to Huntington. We have the negatives, but thought that you would enjoy having the original prints.

I am sorry that we did not have a chance to stop by last weekend. I know your Labor Day party was a success.

Please give your family our best.

Love,

(Their signature)
Barbara and Dudley

PS. John says hello.

After receiving the letter from Barbara, Dudley, Victoria and John, dated February 8, 1974, I of course assumed the event was an indication the family would once again unite. I say "of course" because I am such an optimist. However, this has never reached fruition. Perhaps I saw more in their letter than was present or more than they really meant to say. Yet, our reply might not have been what they wanted or expected. I shall never be certain of the reason for the remaining division, but I know it is ever present.

We later saw and talked with John and Dudley and their families when Mother and Daddy celebrated their fiftieth anniversary on December 29, 1975. However, our actions and speech reflected the uncertainties which continued to exist between us. We exchanged pleasantries, but there were no true indications of love, concern or even kindness. As expected, we kissed and hugged and smiled and returned to Huntington with feelings of disappointment and dejection. During the following years, we met at weddings, holidays and deaths, as do most families, but without sincere emotions or actions. As Dag Hammarskjöld prophesied in his manuscript *Markings* (which he left behind after his death), "Time goes by: reputation increases, ability declines." Is it possible fear and suspicion have destroyed our ability to relate to each other, leaving no hope for reconciliation?

PART V

o o o o o o o o o o o o o o o o o o o o o o o o o o o o o o o o

And it bears the fruit of Deceit,
Ruddy and sweet to eat;
And the raven his nest has made
In its thickest shade.

—Verse 5
"The Human Abstract"
by
William Blake, 1794

10

Stockholders Suit 1975

The rumors concerning certain illegal activities within the Piece Goods Shop, Inc. and the sister corporations started bubbling forth in 1972. However, it was not until October 31, 1975 that nine shareholders filed suit in the U.S. District Court for $5 million actual damages, $5 million punitive damages and the removal of Daddy and my twin brothers Dudley III and John from chain management. The suit accused them of complex frauds in 11 different corporations which they had formed and merged into the chain of 74 Piece Goods Shops throughout the eastern United States.

The Internal Revenue Service had made claim on May 7, 1974, against The Piece Goods Shop, Inc., for unreported income in the form of cash receipts of the corporation and a previous corporation which was taken during the year 1961 (probably the Huntington PGS) through 1972 by Dudley III, then president. The claim by the IRS was for taxes, interest due on the taxes and a fraud penalty. The claims were issued as a result of voluntary disclosures made to the IRS in 1973 by Dudley III concerning the receipts characterized by the IRS as informal dividends. On October 24, 1974, Dudley paid $40,000.00 representing the amount of cash receipts obtained from the corporation. He also deposited into the corporation the additional sum of $15,000.00 that was used to reimburse the corporation for penalties and interest which the corporation might have been charged by the IRS at a later date.

In 1972, after our suit, Barbara and Dudley moved their home to Winston-Salem, North Carolina. This city also became the headquarters of the corporation. The lawsuit of 1975 was filed on behalf of stockholders in West Virginia, Kentucky and North Carolina. They claimed they had been swindled out of at least $500,000.00 in actual losses and an unknown amount in lost profit from 1968 to the date of the suit. The plaintiffs claimed Daddy and my brothers had persuaded them to invest in several different Simms fabric companies, using falsified records to deceive investors. Later other falsified records were used to induce investors to merge the firms into The Piece Goods Shop, Inc. of North Carolina. The suit also claimed the three of them transferred merchandise from stores owned jointly with others to stores owned wholly by the family.

Other allegations made were: (1) Dudley III stole large amounts of money from different PGS stores, destroying sales records and cash register tapes to cover the shortage; (2) Dudley III sold his home in Huntington to the PGS corporation for $165,000.00 when it was worth only $125,000.00, causing the firm a $40,000.00 loss; (3) Dudley III could not continue $20,000.00-a-month premium payments on a personal $1 million life insurance policy, so he had the company pay the premiums and reimburse him for previous payments; (4) Dudley III and John used company funds for remodeling on their private homes and to maintain private condominium apartments in Florida; (5) Dudley III placed a friend on the PGS payroll who did not work for the chain.

In addition, the lawsuit claimed the Simmses personally enriched themselves by submitting "false and grossly overstated personal expense accounts" to the firm. They also falsified inventory records and financial reports, to the Charleston accounting firm of Krisher and Krisher, so to make it appear the stores' profits were less then they in truth were. The suit noted that Dudley III filed a public statement in November 1974, saying he restored $40,000.00 to the corporation at the request of the Internal Revenue Service, to cover funds he removed from 1961 through 1972. But, the stockholders asserted "The wrongful stealing of Corporate monies and assets had continued since 1972, and is continuing."

On November 4, 1975, Daddy and my brothers printed a public notice in various newspapers, denying these allegations. In it they declared that they "categorically and absolutely deny any wrong doings at any time" in the operation of the chain. And, they said, "It is particularly regrettable that such a suit has been filed at a time when the Piece Goods Shop management has produced profits which are at an all-time high and the company's cash position is at an all-time high. The nine plaintiffs in the suit represent a very small fraction of the shareholders of Piece Goods Shop, Inc. These nine plaintiffs are all former franchises who in turn became shareholders of the parent company.

"When similar allegations were first made almost a year ago by the same persons who are plaintiffs in the law suit, the company, through its independent directors, promptly investigated the allegations and made a determination that they were groundless. The independent directors submitted their findings in a detailed report to the plaintiffs and made an offer to the plaintiffs to allow plaintiffs' attorneys and accountants an opportunity to personally inspect company books, records and personnel to determine the truth. Plaintiffs failed to respond either to the report or to the offer of the independent directors.

"The Company especially regrets the attack on the character and integrity of its Chairman Dudley L. Simms, whose record of public service and whose dedication to civic causes are well known throughout the entire country. We are confident that his character and reputation, as well as those of John L. Simms and Dudley L. Simms III, will be vindicated in the course of litigation. In this regard, appropriate pleadings will be filed in due course and the suit will be defended with vigor." In 1978 the company settled for $250,000.00 in the 1975 lawsuit brought by the shareholders who alleged company waste and mismanagement. Later in 1978 Daddy, Dudley III and John bought up the remaining company stock, and the business became private once again.

New York Firm Buys PGS

In 1982 the entire chain of Piece Goods Shop, Inc. was sold to the Jordan Company, a privately owned New York investment-banking firm. The purchase price was not disclosed. The Winston-Salem Journal newspaper printed an article with details concerning the sale on Tuesday, August 24, 1982. They said that "John L. Simms and Dudley Lee Simms III, the twin brothers who founded the business here in 1961 and ran it until last week, will maintain their operations in real estate and other investments. Those operations will become part of Simms Investment, Inc."

The paper also reported there were nearly 100 outlets in nine states which had retail sales of more than $50 million in the last year. The Jordan Company spokesman said they had no plans to change the basic operations. "It has been a pretty successful formula over the years. Changing it would be a little like changing the formula for Coca-Cola." David Zalaznick of The Jordan Company said it is his company's practice to buy a company, leave its operational management intact and work through its board of directors. John Jordan and he worked previously on acquisitions with the Wall Street firm of Carl Marks and Company. Zalaznick and Jordan founded their company in February 1982 and (at the time of the PGS purchase in 1982) controlled 20 companies with combined sales of more than $2 billion.

The article continued, "The Simms brothers took their business concept from their father, who had started a retail fabric store in West Virginia in 1935. The company grew quickly in the '60's and '70's, and it went public in 1972. In 1978 the company settled for $250,000.00 in a 1975 lawsuit brought by stockholders who alleged company waste and mismanagement. Later that year the Simms family bought up the remaining stock and went private again."

After several years, under the ownership of the Jordan Company, The PGS chain was sold to another firm and later it was sold again. The last company that bought the chain has closed most of the shops, if not all of them. The name of this chain was "Mae's." And so ends the family's bold endeavor into the world of enterprise, The Piece Goods Shop, Inc.

My father Dudley Lee Simms, Jr. was able to retain individual ownership of his business in Charleston, West Virginia, until his death in March 1983. Following this, the Executors of his Will chose to liquidate The Charleston Piece Goods Shop located at 710 Lee Street. Thus the raven completed the task and enjoyed the ruddy and sweet fruit of deceit. (See verse five of "The Human Abstract" by William Blake.)

11

Dudley L. Simms, Jr. and family

In the novelette *Delta Wedding* by Eudora Welty, Robbie (a daughter-in-law), attempts to explain her family-by-marriage: "I think you are already the same as what you love. So you couldn't understand. You are just loving yourselves over and over again!...You still love them and they still love you. No matter what you have done to each other!" Although Robbie was describing one family, I believe it describes most families and relationships. We are attracted by what we know, understand and love; we search for the identical characteristics in others. Being a member of my family has always been a privilege and a blessing; I continue to feel this way and I believe I shall always possess these thoughts.

Though Daddy was the founder of the Piece Goods Shop, Mother (Opal M. Riddle) was the power and the strength of the family. She was the one who possessed the ambitions and ideals to build a family that would achieve, and to her this included material wealth as much as a gain of moral and personal status, which would please God and man. She often declared, "When I met your Daddy, I knew he would be a fine husband and father." At an early age, she was aware of what she wanted and how to attain it.

It is my opinion Mother made an excellent choice when she chose my father Dudley Simms, Jr. to become her husband. In fact, if I could have, I would have selected Opal and Dudley as my parents. They were young and beautiful and loved children. When I was born, Mother was eighteen and Daddy nineteen, making them closer to my age than most parent were. For this reason, they were able to relate to me and my thoughts and I to theirs; there was no need for me to explain each of my thoughts or actions to them.

In addition, they were both handsome. When Daddy first met Mother, at Lincoln Junior High School on the West Side of Charleston, Mother was fourteen and he was fifteen; she possessed all the attributes of youth. She was lovely, innocent, happy, and energetic. Her face reminded one of a perfect shaped heart found only in valentines; her eyes were bright blue almonds, and her hair, a smart bobbed cap of light brown streaks. Her body was 5 feet five inches of soft curves. She was a creation for which God could be proud. But God would have approved her also for her spirit and manners. Her actions were interesting, provocative and enjoyable. Yet, all these characteristics appeared natural; they were neither learned nor contrived. She was a product of her ancestors. She was what she was because she could be nothing else.

No one should be surprised that Daddy proposed to her during the summer of 1925, while she was working behind the candy counter at one of the local "five and dime" stores. There is a probability that most of the readers of today do not realize what type of stores these are as there are none exactly like these remaining in today's society. "Five and dimes" were also called "dime stores." The most popular were Kresges, McCroys, and Woolworths. These shops marketed articles which usually were priced under one dollar. They always had a candy counter where the candy (or nuts) were weighed and bagged; the product was not pre-packaged. Some dime stores even had lunch counters and piano players to present the latest sheet music for the local customers. They also marketed inexpensive jewelry, hair products, hose, socks, accessories for the home, cosmetics, sundries; in fact, if the article could be sold for less than 100 pennies, the customer could find it in such stores. And, it was in one of the shops that my mother worked.

Daddy often came in the store and visited with her; he may have even sampled a few of the chocolates, but one visit was different from all the others. During this extraordinary visit, Dudley asked Opal Marie Riddle to marry him. I can't imagine how he phrased the question, but she answered, "Yes." He had even purchased the ring; it was an etched white gold mounting set with a respectable diamond. I am able to describe the ring in detail as Mother wore it until it was replaced with a ring set with a larger stone. In addition, when Sean, our third son, fell in love with his wife-to-be Laura Deveny, this ring became the engagement ring; and I expect it will remain in our family.

Now to return to my reasons for being pleased with my parents. I have said they were young, beautiful and loved children. Well, Daddy was not lovely, but he was handsome. He was five feet, nine inches tall and of medium weight. He had brown hair with a reddish tint to it and brown eyes, which reflected his pleasant personality. His face was round (and so is mine). Many people say I favor him in appearance. However, my eyes are blue like Mother's. I was their only child with blue eyes. Betty Lee (my lone sister) and my brothers Dudley and John (whom you have met) inherited Daddy's deep brown eyes. Furthermore, Daddy was good-tempered, fair, responsible, hard-working, slow to provoke and fastidious. He loved playing pool and was an above-average player. Hoping to always have a game, he taught all of us to play. When he became more successful financially, he bought a Brunswick table for the game room. Betty Lee became an outstanding player; she often challenged her dates to play and would win without mercy for her opponents. But I am losing my focus. Daddy enjoyed watching all sports, but his favorite was baseball.

The third reason for being pleased with my parents was their affection for children. There was not a moment I doubted their love, not even when they refused to see me or talk to me during the period of the suit. I can't say I know the true reason for their actions during the 1971 suit, but placing the blame on a lack of love is ludicrous. Mother and Daddy often expressed their love for me, and I have always declared my love for them. Being an outwardly affectionate family, we kissed and embraced each other physically, spoke of our devotion verbally and demonstrated our emotions through words, attention and gifts. I have kept many of the letters and cards that they sent to us, and our home and lives have been blessed by their caring and generous gifts.

Even at an early age, Daddy was ambitious, just as Mother was, only his desires were not as consuming or as materialistic. Daddy came from a large family of eight girls and two boys. However, his older brother died in 1920, when Daddy was a boy of twelve. My grandfather Dudley L. Simms, Sr. owned a general store in London, West Virginia, where Daddy was born on November 8, 1908. London is a small community about 20 miles east of Charleston. The building where Grandfather Simms had his business was visible from Route 60. The name Simms was painted in large letters on the side. As a young child, I remember seeing the remains of our name, while we were enjoying our Sunday drives.

When Daddy was two, the family moved to a house on Maryland Avenue in Charleston. His parents lived there until the death of his father and mother in 1932. Later the house was occupied by two of his sisters, Evelyn Pittman and Margaret Mitter, and their families. In 1904, my Grandfather Simms became a traveling salesman for the Elk Milling and Produce Company. He appeared to excel financially. He owned a large home and a Pierce Arrow touring automobile, fed and clothed a family of twelve plus other relatives, was an active member of Calvary Baptist Church, and sent my father to Greenbrier Military School.

In fact, Daddy was attending Greenbrier when he wrote this letter to my mother on September 24, 1925. Mother had just reached sixteen, and he would become seventeen on November 8.

Greenbrier Military School
Lewisburg, W. Va.
Sept. 24, 1925

Dear Sweetheart,

We didn't go to school but a half a day today but I didn't go any for I was helping to fix up the football field for the game this afternoon.

We sure had a funny experience on the field this morning and then not so funny after all. Captain Joe Moore, myself and a few more boys were just finishing the field and there came a bull across the yard and Captain Joe and another boy went over to head it off so it wouldn't tear down the ropes we had put up. But the bull was mad and started after the boy. Captain Joe knew if the bull would catch him, it would likely hurt him very bad, so he went over and hit it. Then the bull started to chase him and he had to run. It then started after us. I jumped over a five-foot fence, farther than I had ever jumped in my life. The other couldn't quite get over the fence so I helped him over. We sure did have some time there for awhile. I do not know where it came from but a man came and got it. Believe me I don't want to be in a scrap like that one again.

So you like the...

(The last part of the letter was missing.)

There was another letter that I discovered, but, even though it was not dated, I believed it was written before their marriage. The top of the stationery was imprinted with Pittsburgh Wheeling Coal Company. (Granddaddy Simms's brother O.T. Simms lived in Wheeling. Perhaps, Daddy was visiting him.) Daddy began with the following heading.

Monday Morning

130 Edgewood St.
Wheeling, W.Va.

Dear Little Girl,

You will have to excuse the writing as well as the contents of this letter as I have had no occasion till now of writing a real friendly letter. As you know I hated to leave but it couldn't be helped as I knew I was coming back as soon as possible. I didn't sleep much last night. I was tired, lonesome and blue. I was on the train in a car with a lot of baseball players and show people so you know what a noise they made all night.

I sure do miss you and our friends although you and your mother are the greatest. Tell them hello for me. I don't know what I would do if it wasn't for the pictures of you and the house to look at.

I sure did appreciate your coming to the train yesterday. It was certainly a great surprise for me. Thank Harvey and Gwen for me for bringing you although I know it was a great effort on your part.

I had to wait in Huntington two hours and forty-five minutes last night and wanted to call you but I couldn't get your house. I don't know how long I am going to stay but I hope not long. I don't believe I will ever forget the day I left.

What did you do last night? You didn't two-time me did you? I would of given the world to of been there instead on that old train. Watch your company and not too many car rides, remember, I will be back soon.

How was the pictures we took Sunday. Send me a picture of each or the negatives including the two that Gwen has, if you could be so nice.

Has Ivan and Glenna made up yet? I think they will. Has the Polings come back from Ohio yet? Tell Clark and Ivan to write me and most of all your mother.

When are you going down to your Aunt Bertha's. Tell her good-bye for me as I was very sorry I didn't get to see her before I left. How do you feel not working? Do you care? I don't, I am sure.

I am expecting a big letter from you any minute now. Don't put off answering a minute as you have nothing to do now. I'll answer as soon as I get yours.

With oceans of true love which shall never end.

Dudley

P.S. This is the only way I can express my love for you now so we will have to make the best of it. XOXOXO

I would guess the previous letter was written during the summer of 1925. Daddy attended Greenbrier Academy the following fall and returned home for the Christmas break. On December 29, 1925, Mother and Daddy caught a train to Greenup, Kentucky, were married, then returned to their separate lives. The marriage was announced the following summer. Mother was sixteen and Daddy was seventeen.

On January 31, 1926, Daddy wrote Mother a letter that she received on Sunday, February 2, 1926. It was mailed Special Delivery and cost ten cents. Mother signified, by writing on the envelope, that this was the twentieth letter she had received and she gave it a rating of "good." The words, Greenbrier Military School were printed on the first line and Lewisburg, West Virginia on the second line.

Dear Wife,

Sorry you did not receive any letter Friday but you should have for I mailed it in time. I gave it to a man to mail in Ronceverte Thursday afternoon.

The Litany Societies met this afternoon. They met separate today. We had a very good program. I've never been on one of the programs as yet. Jack has been making out the programs and that's the reason. I hope I never come on but I will have to before long.

I am in Company C now and it's not so bad. It's a better Company than I expected. One reason I hated to go to "C" is they haven't had such a good basketball team and I will have to play with them.

It is reported here that we lost to Huntington last night. The score was 36 to 28. If the report is right, that's too bad. They play Ashland tonight and I hope they have better luck. There won't be any game here tonight and I will probably go to the show or stay at school. This is town afternoon but I don't believe I will go.

I heard one boy went blind and another insane on poison whiskey in Charleston. That certainly is awful, but they should of left it alone. Maybe some people will take it as a warning and stay away from the "moonshine."

Honey, just think that this time last week I was with the sweetest little one in all the world, my own little wife. I wish you were here now. I miss you, oh dear, so very much. I think and dream of you constantly. Nothing could ever take you off my mind for I love you a great big lots and only you. If I could only see you every day I would be so happy.

Be real good, write everyday and keep all promises; with all my love and my hearts best, forever.

Love

Hubby

XOXOXOXOX etc.

Another letter was written on Friday and mailed February 5, 1926, from Lewisburg, West Virginia.

Dear Wife,

Received your letter this noon and certainly glad to get it as I always am. But, oh! how much happier I would be if I was only with you.

I'm so very, very lonesome for my little wife. I miss you so much for I love you a big whole lots, more than that. The time seems to go so slow without my dear, Opal, and it is awful blue without you. If the time doesn't go faster I don't know what I will do.

I couldn't do without your letters. They mean so much to me. I look forward everyday for them. I get an awful lot of pleasure reading them.

We went to study hall this afternoon. We had all our classes this morning. Study hall lasted from two o'clock until three thirty. The Lyceum Course is tonight and I do hope it is interesting. I hate to sit through them when they aren't a bit interesting. I like them when they are but would rather be in school when they are not.

Mrs. Lacy the wife of the founder of this school was buried today. Some of the cadets went to the funeral, Mr. Lacy has been dead for some time. Of course he didn't start the first school here but the one which is here now. There has been a school for boys here since 1808. One hundred and eighteen years ago there was a school here. It use to go under the name of Greenbrier Presbyterian School.

It has about stopped snowing now but the snow is sticking fine.

There was suppose to of been two basketball games here tonight but on account of the Lyceum Course, they will be played tomorrow night.

Jack and I went back to bed this morning after reveille and stayed until inspection. That's the first time I ever went back to bed after reveille but I was so tired, cold and sleepy.

Honey, I will have to stop and mail this letter for it is nearly five now.

Be good, keep all promises, and write everyday.

Love forever

Dudley

XOXOXOXOX etc.
millions more
for my sweetheart!
my love

Strange though it may seem, I know very little about what Daddy did during his months at the Academy. From the time I was a little girl, I can remember going by the school and through those gates that had been left unlocked. Daddy would show where he had lived, marched and practiced sports. He also bragged about a small business he had while there. He would take the soiled clothes of those who did not wish to walk to town, deliver them to be cleaned, return to the cleaners, gather the clean garments and carry them back to the owners. For this he received a nominal fee; he enjoyed the money and the opportunity. We also visited the church that the cadets were required to attend. Wearing their long military blue wool coats with brass buttons and capes lined with bright red flannel, they would march together down the middle of the street, chanting. This was a tradition that remained until the school closed in the 1970's; during this time, the school administration was forced to choose between losing their ROTC program or integrating. The school was not integrated; the ROTC program was disbanded; the Greenbrier Military Academy was closed. A state orthopedic college now replaces the school. This does not signify our never visiting the area again. In fact, we never pass within five miles of the previous school grounds without driving through and around what was Greenbrier Military School. Keith and I have taken our children, even our grandchildren, on this excursion and I would say there is not one child who is not more proficient in directing the tour than we are. Of course, our family has other ties besides Daddy's with the school. My brothers Dudley and John, my nephew John Sears, and our son Robert Sean attended Greenbrier. It is a part of our family history.

There is one more letter that Mother gave to me that Daddy wrote during the Greenbrier School period. The letter is proof that my father was learning and maturing. This letter begins with a complete heading.

Greenbrier Military School
Lewisburg, W.Va.
April 14, 1925

My Dear Wife,

Received your letter today and certainly was glad to get it. Honey, I don't know what I'd do without you and your precious letters. I wait eagerly for your letters each day and am terrible disappointed when I don't receive any. If I only got enough of your letters to read all day probably I wouldn't get so lonesome and blue. But as it is I can hardly stay here because I'm so lonesome and miss you so much. I think of my little wife, which I left back in Charleston, all the time and wonder if she is as lonesome as I am, and misses me as much as I do her. I love you oh! So much, and it just thrills me to think I have such a sweet little girl for my wife. A wife that anyone would be proud of and I certainly am proud of you.

The baseball team is playing Augusta Military Academy this afternoon at Augusta. I hope they win the game and I expect they will.

We didn't have a dress parade yesterday. The grounds were too wet. I knew when I didn't have to go to them the parade would be called off for some reason. We are supposed to have one tomorrow and if the weather doesn't change the grounds will be in good shape for it.

The Faculty Baseball team is playing the second team this afternoon and I bet it will be a hot game. Today is town day but I think I'll stay and see the game.

Dear, remember that I love you all I possibly can, and no matter what I am doing I'm always thinking of the one I love, "my darling wife."

Be real good. Keep all promises and write everyday.

Love,

Dudley

XOXOXOXOX etc.
     when
     we
     are
     together

Most private schools end in May, so I assume Daddy returned to Charleston by train around May 20. It is difficult to imagine his homecoming. He was probably met by his father and a few of his sisters. I can't visualize his mother being among the group as his mother remained so close to the house. Her responsibilities were many. I do know Daddy started working in 1926 at McGibbons-Demings Department Store located on Capitol Street. I was born on September 11, 1927, and my sister Betty Lee on October 20, 1929, during the crash of the stock market. The depression which followed affected the department store sales, so the owners slowly terminated the department managers. Daddy became the manager for seven departments on the first floor. These departments included shoes, gloves, and yard goods. Later the store was forced into receivership and Daddy was placed in charge of the closing sale. The experience he received was invaluable.

By the time Demings had closed, Mother and Daddy had decided to open a yard goods shop at 702 Lee Street (at the time called State Street). The year was 1935. The new business was named The Piece Goods Shop. He hired two ladies who had worked in yard goods at Demings (Ada Foley and Mae Holbrook), bought the measuring machines and some tables, and traveled to New York City hoping to buy merchandise on credit from manufacturers he had met previously. That plan did not materialize. He then approached some Jewish wholesalers who had enough faith in his ability and integrity to accept his promise to pay later. Our family has always been grateful. These owners, without a doubt, helped our family to achieve a lifestyle and to pursue opportunities beyond our imaginations. The slogan in the beginning was "It pays to shop around the corner." The shop was located around the corner from Capitol Street. As other stores were added to the company, the slogan was changed to "Dress better for less." The second store was opened in Beckley by Daddy and a friend Roland Hinkley in 1945. The third store opened in Parkersburg in 1947. His partners were Georgia and Jim Butner. Georgia (Tootsie) is one of my mother's sisters and Jim, her husband. In 1954, they added another PGS in Marietta, Ohio. The Huntington PGS was opened by Keith and me in 1949. Then Mr. Hinkley opened another shop in 1950 at Bluefield.

Daddy did not open any other stores until Dudley and John entered the business, as he had become very involved in Lions Club International. He joined the Charleston club in 1937 and served as local president in 1941-2. After continuing through the state offices, he was elected to the Lions International Board of Directors in 1951, third Vice President in 1955, and in 1958 he became the International President.

The convention that year was held in Chicago, Illinois. It was a very exciting experience. Keith and I were living in Huntington, and Keith was a Lion in the local club. All of the family members attended the ceremonies. Several car companies offered to allow the family to drive company cars to Chicago. We were asked to drive a blue Dodge convertible. Betty Lee and her husband Jack Sears drove with us. We stayed at the Palmer House. Our Governor Cecil Underwood and his wife Hovah came to represent our state. All of us were so proud of them and of our parents. Daddy was the first and only West Virginian to serve in this position.

There were other organizations in which Daddy was active. He was president of Stonewall Jackson PTA, Charleston Chamber of Commerce, Greenbrier Military School Alumni, exalted ruler of the Elks, a 32nd degree Mason and a Shriner. He served in the United Fund, Red Cross, and the Savings Bond Drives. He raised funds for hospitals and colleges. In addition, he was an active member of the Baptist Temple in Charleston.

He even did a broadcast for Radio Free Europe behind the Iron Curtain. During this program, he had a 45 minute interview with President Eisenhower. And, a few of the dignitaries with whom he visited were Chian Kai-shek of Nationalist China, the Shah of Iran, and Prince Rainer III of Monaco. When discussing Lions International, he was quoted as saying, "As Lions we have come to believe it is not enough that we pay our just taxes or debts or present to the world a well-ordered life. Unless our citizenship has cost us something, life becomes of no avail. Lionism also teaches a man that he owes more to prosperity than simply leaving civilization just where he found it. It teaches a man he has no moral right to bask in the sunlight of what his ancestors did without making some contributions himself." Here is a man who lived his convictions.

Shortly after Daddy finished his term as President of Lions International, he approached Keith and me about the problems at the Huntington PGS. He told us that Keith should resign before the business was declared bankrupt. Following the departure, Keith had several jobs and at one time he had five different ones. I returned to Marshall and finished my AB in Secondary Education with majors in Spanish, English and Social Studies. Keith was able to obtain a position in the finance department at Huntington City Hall. And, in the fall of 1964, I fortunately received a position at Huntington High School, teaching Spanish and history. I had never planned to be a teacher, but no other career could have been as rewarding. I am certain God was the instigator, but he had a little help form my next door neighbor Virginia Dial. She was aware of our struggle with seven bodies to feed and clothe. One morning while sitting on the back porch steps, she leaned over to me and asked, "Why don't you study education at Marshall?" And so I did. That has to be one of the more intelligent decisions of my life. Marshall and the instructors were truly sent from God, whether they knew it or not. Moreover, I have always loved school and all its trappings. But, none of this would have materialized without the help and support of Keith and our children, Tia, Karry, Scott, Sean, and Dirk.

PART VI

o o o o o o o o o o o o o o o o o o o o o o o o o o o o o o o

The Gods of the earth and sea
Sought through Nature to find this Tree;
But their search was all in vain:
There grows one in the Human Brain.

—Verse 6
"The Human Abstract"
by
William Blake

12

Death and Dying

In the later part of the 1960's, Daddy started having severe night sweats. He went to the hospital several times, but no cause was discovered. Later Mother decided to enter Charleston Memorial Hospital for a series of tests and vitamin injections. She planned to be there several days. The hospital had just opened a suite for husbands and wives. Therefore, as Daddy had a small hernia which he was ignoring, Mother asked, "Dudley, is there any reason why you can't go to the hospital at the same time as I do and have the hernia problem corrected?" I couldn't believe he agreed to go, but he did. Daddy had no trouble with the operation itself, but he was given too much anesthetic. The recovery was slow; in fact, he never truly recovered. He acquired rheumatoid arthritis. Upon leaving the hospital, he was forced to use a wheelchair, as he was not able to walk. He could not even feed himself. He then entered the hospital at the University of Virginia in Charlottesville, Virginia. He remained there for at least six weeks. Mother stayed in local motels, and several times my sister or I traveled to Charlottesville to help her. One Sunday, Mother and I had taken Daddy to a restaurant for lunch. He was not able to eat alone and some of the food oozed out of the corner of his mouth. We cleaned it off, but a small amount had dripped on his tie. Here was a man who had been in charge of every phase of his life until the operation. With tears in his eyes, he declared, "You should put me on display. I am now a clown."

Bit by bit, he improved enough to return home. With exercise and medication he again was able to walk by himself and go to the shop, but he never again walked or worked with the assurance and dignity he had possessed before. By 1971, at the time of the suit, he was much improved, but remained a shadow of the person he was before the operation. This was one reason why the family threats concerning Daddy's health were seriously considered by Keith and me. And, in the deposition, when he repeatedly declared, "I do not remember," his statement appeared valid.

Dudley and John directed the business of the chain and its subsidiaries. Daddy worked in the Charleston store. Yet Mother and Daddy were able to travel to Florida in the winter, to New York, Alaska, Europe, to anyplace they desired to visit. Mrs. Parsons (a loyal and faithful employee) managed the store when Daddy was not in Charleston. This arrangement appeared to please all concerned.

However, there was another physical development. As I said previously, Daddy loved cigars. He didn't really enjoy smoking them as much as he did chewing on them or holding them in his mouth. Also, his favorite drink was White Horse Scotch. Later tests showed that this brand of Scotch contained a carcinogen. Thus, with the Scotch and the tobacco, Daddy acquired a small growth on his tongue which was diagnosed as cancerous. After treatments in Charleston, he returned to the University of Virginia hospital. The doctors were able to cure the cancer, but they warned him the cure would perhaps shorten his life. The decision was between quantity or quality, and he chose quality.

During the same time period, Mother began having problems with her health. They assumed it was an ulcer, when, in actuality, it was an adhesion in the intestines. Several years earlier Mother had harmed her pancreas by her use of alcohol. This condition was not discovered until after she had been a patient at Fellowship Hall in North Carolina. Following the diagnosis, she began taking a medication to aid in the digestion and absorption of the foods she ate. Nevertheless, she became thin and weak, no matter how much she ate. Then, when she developed these terrible pains in her abdomen, the doctors refused to consider an alternative affliction. Regardless, until her death, Mother believed she would recover, and so did we. Her lawyer told my sister Betty that, if he had thought she was dying, he would have brought her last will to the hospital for her to sign.

The last time Daddy was downstairs for a meal was the day following Thanksgiving, 1982. After celebrating Thanksgiving with our family at Laura and Sean's farm in Nestlow Hollow, Keith and I drove to "401" to spend the weekend with Mother and Daddy. A fellow Lion's Club member had sent my parents some raw peanuts. On Thanksgiving evening, while we were conversing, I ate some of the nuts. During the night I became extremely ill. I made an attempt to stay for brunch the next morning, but I was in excruciating pain. Keith said to me, "There is nothing else to do but to call Dr. Clay." Dr. Clay had been our doctor in Huntington since we moved there in 1949, so he was the person I most wanted to see. Keith called, giving Dr. Clay the information; he suggested we meet him at the Cabell-Huntington Hospital. When we left the house, Daddy was seated at the table. It was the last time he ate at the table downstairs in the dining room. The next day, Mother was able to hire a male nurse to care for him during the day, and he was served his meals upstairs.

Keith and I returned to Huntington, meeting Dr. Clay at the hospital. After he examined me, he announced, "Patty, your gall bladder will have to be removed, but first we must completely clean out your system. I want you to spend the weekend in the hospital, and then on Monday we shall have the operation. I imagine you will remain here for at least five days after the operation." I could not believe he would force me to remain in the hospital over the weekend, so I asked, "Would it be possible for me to go home over the weekend? I have so much to do." The truth was I had taken a two years leave of absence to complete a doctorate in education and I was finishing my dissertation. I planned to defend it in March and graduate in May. I was also working as a graduate assistant. In addition, the holidays were fast approaching and everyone knew what that entailed, especially when one considered the size family with which we had been blessed. Without blinking, Dr. Clay answered, "I've known you for almost thirty-five years (It was really thirty-three.), and I would not consider your going home. Besides, I know you wouldn't return." Well, at least I tried. Right then and there, I vowed that my next doctor would not know me quite so well. Of course, you realize I am joking. Dr. Clay was a wonderful doctor and friend. Everyone should have such a caring physician.

Do I need to tell you that I did not go home and I did have the operation? At this time, there was no laser surgery; thus, after the operation, I was flat on my back with all these tubes and needles extending from my body. I do remember being extracted from the bed by giants dressed in white and being coerced into pushing my feet and legs across the hospital floor, with one giant on each side. (Why do I think this occurred within the first twenty-four hours?) In addition, these giants used such motivating remarks as, "Don't be such a baby." I remember thinking that dying in Charleston might have been a better choice.

A few days after the operation, while I remained flat on my back and decorated with tubes and needles, I heard the click of high heels on the terrazzo floor of the hospital hall. I clearly recognized my mother's steps. She appeared at my door, dressed in her usual elegance. This day she was wearing a black velvet suit, a white silk crepe blouse, a gold coin on a chain around her neck, and two gold charm bracelets. In her hand, she held a lovely container of Estee Lauder dusting powder, a gift for me. Reaching over the rails of what-I-felt-was my casket, she kissed my cheek and remarked, "Losing that weight certainly becomes you." An appropriate reply would have been, "Thank you, but I must appear better than I feel." Of course, I did not answer in such a fashion. I was pleased to see her, as I realized the effort and energy the visit cost her. She was not well and was confined to her bed shortly afterward.

Christmas 1982 was not one of our best. I returned home from the hospital around December 10. Keith decorated the tree and house by himself, while I directed. His mother came from Illinois around December 15 for the holidays and remained until shortly after Christmas.

Dudley, John and their families visited Mother and Daddy after Christmas, and Mother managed to leave her bed and to dress properly for a tea dance at the Edgewood Country Club. I have a picture of her in her silk organza and taffeta formal,which substantiated her physical condition. Daddy remained in his room during the entire holiday.

By February 1983, Mother had been admitted to Charleston Memorial Hospital. At first, she was treated for ulcers, but she did not respond favorably. Thus, the doctor or doctors decided to do a exploratory operation. It was discovered she had an obstruction in her intestines; however, she was not strong enough to recover from the procedure. She remained on machines in intensive care for approximately a week. During this period, I would visit Daddy at "401." One day, near the end of Mother's earthly life, he said, "Dudley and John say your mother is improving, but I feel she is dying. I know you will not lie to me. Tell me the truth." Thus, I did what I believed was the right action. "Daddy, I hate telling you, but all our prayers and hopes do not seem to affect her condition. She appears to be near the end," I confessed.

A few days before her death Dudley and John rented an ambulance. They had the nurse dress Daddy in his latest custom-made suit, shirt, tie, overcoat and felt hat. They then drove with him to Charleston Memorial Hospital, placed him in a wheel chair which was situated on the walk under the window of the room where Mother was being kept and then directed Daddy's attention to that area. I have never known what they said to him or their purpose for Daddy's visit, but I am certain they felt it was as near a last reunion for Mother and Daddy as they were able to create.

Mother's death was listed as February 23, 1983; most of us considered it as occurring on the day of the operation. But, whatever the date was, it was the saddest experience I have ever had. I realize this is a selfish statement, but it is what I honestly feel. I have missed her ever since. During one of her stays in the hospital, I brought her a magazine among other gifts, hoping to offer her a few moments of enjoyment.

While turning the pages, she inquired, "Why is it you're the only one that truly understands me?" I can't remember how I responded; I probably kissed her. Even though others may have understood her, I believe our relationship was beyond that of a mother and a daughter, of even two humans. We loved and appreciated each other. We were and are kindred spirits.

Six days later Daddy died. The date was March 1, 1983. Mother had often claimed that Daddy (though he had been confined longer) would not die before she had left this world. Daddy attended Mother's funeral, returned to his room and bed. He was able to visit with a few family members during the gathering held at "401," following the ceremony. Dudley and John actually planned Mother's service. It was held in the sanctuary at the Baptist Temple on Quarrier Street in Charleston. Without a doubt, Mother attended the affair from Heaven with pleasure and pride.

The service opened with prelude music by the West Virginia Brass Quintet, then a vocal solo of "Softly and Tenderly" accompanied by the violin. Everyone attending sang "Fairest Lord Jesus," followed by the invocation and a tribute to Mother given by my brother John. Next, solos of "There's a Sweet, Sweet Spirit," "Amazing Grace," "The Lord's Prayer" (sung by my uncle H. Kenneth Andrews, husband of Mother's sister Stachia), "Let's Just Praise the Lord," and "Because He Lives." Scripture readings were given between the musical selections. Dr. Fish (the pastor) presented the message "Good Grief" and the service ended with "Christ the Lord Is Risen" and "God of our Fathers." The grandsons were the ushers.

The sanctuary was filled with family and friends from West Virginia and other states. My family was placed behind the pews of Dudley's, John's and Betty's, as were our names on the program. I can't say that I truly cared, but it was so obvious that people still remind me of it. However, the service was in honor of Mother; it was not about me. Mother's casket was covered with a blanket of pale pink roses, something she had said she wanted. The burial occurred at Sunset Memorial

Park in Spring Hill, near South Charleston. Mother would have approved.

All of us returned home to our daily activities. I was working in the education office at Marshall when one of my daughter-in-laws called on the following Tuesday to tell me of my father's death. He was watching the morning news on television and reading the *Charleston Gazette* (his two favorite pastimes) when he looked at his nurse, smiled and raised his hand. The nurse said it was as if he were leaving on a trip. He was packed and ready; there was no reason to linger. The date was March 1, 1983. He was seventy-four years old; Mother was seventy-three.

The service was almost identical to Mother's except the tribute was presented by John Stickley (a close friend and fellow Lion from North Carolina) and Dr. Fish, the pastor, gave the message, "Our Shepherd's There." Friends and Lions came from far and wide to honor Daddy. His casket was covered with a blanket of red roses. I did not view Daddy's body before he was buried, as my brothers showed their disapproval so vehemently when I viewed Mother's. The services were held with closed caskets, of which I approved, but the viewing seemed (to me) to be a private good-bye. Daddy was dressed in a new Hickey Freeman suit with a red tie to coordinate with the lining of the casket, or so I was told. Mother's sister Stachia and James Butner (the husband of Mother's youngest sister Georgia) were not permitted to view Daddy's body either. They did go to the funeral home and waited for Dudley and John to return to give permission for the funeral directors to open the casket, but they never arrived. I pray that Daddy doesn't think we should have pursued the right to view his body, but knowing Daddy, I believe he would understand and perhaps be amused somewhat at the cost of the burial ensemble with matching casket lining and no one seeing it but the employees of Wison Funeral Home.

Each culture has its own practices concerning death and dying. When I was a young girl, the dead were dressed in their finery and laid in the casket. This act was not based on a premise that the spirit remained in the body. Those who wished to do so would view the body or even touch it. To me, it was an expression of love and respect. Not everyone would agree, but agreement is not necessary. My viewing Mother privately at the funeral home upset my brothers. Daddy's death was so close to Mother's I decided not to visit Daddy as I felt it would add to the many emotional problems in evidence at this time. I always felt Mother and Daddy were handsome people from whom I had received joy and love; seeing both of them one more time as they had appeared on earth would have given me pleasure. However, being aware of Dudley and John's possible reactions, I declined to visit Daddy. My pleasure was not worth the risk of causing more pain to others.

Mother and Daddy were buried side by side. My sister Betty Lee's sons Brent and John were born into the family business of Sears Monument Company, so they were capable of assuring the creation of markers and monuments which would enhance the burial. The marble used was a deep rose color. On Daddy's marker, there appeared his name, his date of birth (November 8, 1908) and the date of his death (March 1, 1983). Under this was inscribed:

MARRIED 57 YEARS—DIED SIX DAYS APART
INTERNATIONAL PRESIDENT OF LIONS

And, above Daddy's name was

THANK YOU FOR JESUS GIFT FOR SALVATION. D.L.S.

Mother's marker was created of identical marble and was inscribed with:

DEATH PUT OUT THE LAMP
BECAUSE THE DAWN HAS COME
OPAL M. RIDDLE SIMMS
SEPT. 5, 1909 FEB 23, 1983
MARRIED 57 YEARS—DIED SIX DAYS APART

I LOVE YOU AND JESUS DOES TOO. O.M.S.
WE MAY BE OLD BUT WE ARE WORTH SAVING. O.M.S.

The sentence relating to Jesus was one she wrote on cards and letters. The last sentence was what she often repeated to doctors while Daddy and she were so ill. Dr. Scaggs, their physician for years, had retired, and she was bothered by the lack of concern and care of the younger doctors. I wondered if their attitudes and treatment were due to their failing to acquire the appropriate training and skills. Whatever was the cause, they both died, were buried, and markers were placed at each grave. A monument, designed by Dudley III and John, was also erected on the plot. It was and is approximately forty inches across and five and a half feet tall. In the center is a huge stone that resembles a rock on which is inscribed, front and back, the family name SIMMS. On each end of the stone are two columns which appear to be broken near the top. A dove is etched on the left column and a cross on the right one. On the base is inscribed:

JESUS SAID, "COME FOLLOW ME."
MATT. 4:19.

The monument is fashioned from the identical marble as the markers.

Before Dudley died, he told me the significance of the broken columns. He said they depicted the ends of Mother and Daddy's lives on earth. The dove represented the Living Spirit of Jesus and the cross, Christ's saving grace. Of course, neither Mother nor Daddy were able to view the monument, but I believe they would approve of the selection as it reflects their beliefs, their spirits, their lives on earth and their love.

Mother's Will was dated April 17, 1982. The witnesses were three persons from Winston-Salem, North Carolina, or in the area. Item III designated who would receive her personal property. Betty Lee was given Mother's nutria coat and I, her mink coat. John received all of her gold charm bracelets; Dudley, her gold coin bracelets. Mother also noted that the twelve place settings of Dresden china and a diamond ring which belonged to Betty were to be returned to Betty. She stated that Betty Lee was to return a diamond ring of one carat to Dudley III. The rest of her tangible personal property (including jewelry, silverware, glassware, china, tableware, linen and figurines owned by her at the time of her death) was to be divided among Betty, Dudley III and John. In addition, all of the furniture, furnishings, appliances and other tangible personal properties were to be divided among them, unless Daddy was still living at the time of her death. If this did happen (as it did), the furnishings were to remain in the house until his death and then be divided equally.

In item IV, my brother John inherited the house, in trust for Daddy who was to remain there during his lifetime without being required to give bond and without paying rent, but he was required to pay all taxes, assessments and insurance. There was a provision made to allow Daddy to sell the house if he wished to make other living arrangements. Upon his death or remarriage (after Mother's death), the Trustee was to allow Betty to live in the house or to use the income from the sale of the house or its replacement for as long as she lived or until her remarriage. If Betty chose to live at "401," the Trustees were to collect from her the money to pay property taxes, insurance and repairs. When she died or remarried, the residence was to be sold and the proceeds equally divided between Tracy Sears (Betty's daughter), Troy, Tuesdy, Tracy, and Dudley Simms IV (Dudley's children), and Jay and Alannah Simms (John's children). Neither my children nor Betty's two sons were to receive any of the proceeds. If John Simms failed to qualify as her Trustee, Dudley III was to be Substitute Trustee. If neither of them qualified, Robert Bias (Dudley's friend who lived in Huntington) was to become her Trustee.

In items V and VI, any capital stock which she may have owned at the time of her death in The Piece Goods Shops, Inc. or in any successor corporation was to be divided between Dudley III and John. All the rest, residue and remainder of her estate and property, real and personal, money, stock, bonds, insurance proceeds, et cetera, was to go to Daddy (if he were still living) to be his absolutely. If Daddy predeceased her, died with her, or did not survive her by as many as thirty days, all of the property in item VI would be bequeath to Betty, Dudley III, and John, to share and share alike.

The next item (VII) pertained to me. It stated, "I make no provision in this Will for my daughter Patricia Harrison or her issue, except as specifically provided, because I have contributed liberally to their upkeep and maintenance, and I consider that as a result they have already received what I meant for them to have. I specifically provide that my said daughter, Patricia Harrison, her husband and her children are not to participate in my estate in any way except as may be specifically provided."

Daddy's Will was similar to Mother's. It was signed by Daddy on June 14, 1978, four years before Mother's Will and seven years after the suit. Mother had a previous will, but Mother's Winston-Salem Will was written because (as of 1982) Daddy was expected to die before Mother and the boys wanted to be assured of their inheritances, or at least this is what was told to me. Item I covered Debts and Taxes. Item 2.I related to Tangible Personal Property, which was to go to Mother if she survived Daddy. If not, Betty, Dudley and John were to share the personal items. The assets of The Charleston PGS were not included. Corporate Stocks were treated in Item 2.2. If Mother lived beyond Daddy, she was to receive the stocks; if not, Dudley and John were to be given any capital stock he may have owned at the time of his death in The Piece Goods Shop, Inc., a North Carolina corporation, or any successor corporation. Residence property (2.2) was to be Betty's, if Mother did not survive him. (This differed from Mother's Will.) I was mentioned in 2.3 under Payment or Forgiveness of Indebtedness. It stated, "I hereby forgive any indebtedness of my daughter, Patricia Harrison, or any of her children, to me, at the date of my death; and I further provide that my Executors shall pay any indebtedness of my said daughter or of any of her children existing at the date of my death which I have endorsed or guaranteed. (With our copy of the Will were two notes that Keith and I had given to Daddy.) One was dated June 25, 1949 and signed by Keith only. The amount was six thousand dollars. On May 21, 2001, while reviewing research for this book, Keith and I were guessing why he alone signed this note, and we decided it was probably the note for the 40 shares of PGS Huntington stock. 40 X $150.00 per share (the price listed) would equal $6,000.00. The other note was for seven thousand dollars and dated October 28, 1949. Keith and I both signed this one. We surmised it was the down payment for our house at "1016." During December 1949, Keith and I became responsible for the $10,000.00 mortgage. In 1955 we added an addition to the house and refinanced the loan for $15,000.00. About this time, Daddy signed the papers over to us; the mortgage was paid in full, by us, in the fall of 1983.

Daddy, in Item III, left the residue to Mother, if she still lived at the time of his death. If not Betty, Dudley III and John would inherit the residue, and, in the case of one of them predeceasing him, the spouse and/or issue of Daddy's deceased child would inherit that person's share. (The rest of this section is not really pertinent as Mother and Daddy have died and the Wills have been executed.)

In the third part of Item III, Daddy said, "I make no provision in this Will for my daughter Patricia Harrison or her issue, except in paragraph 2.4 hereof, because I have contributed liberally to their upkeep and maintenance, and I consider that as a result they have received a fair share of my estate. I especially provide that my said daughter, Patricia Harrison, her husband, and her children are not to participate in my estate in any way except as may be provided in paragraph 2.4 of this Will, or in any codicil to this Will."

Appointment of Executors was brought forth in Item IV. Daddy nominated and appointed Mother, Dudley III, John and Betty Lee, or those of them who survived him and were residents of West Virginia. Next the powers of the executors were established. The Charleston

PGS was then discussed as it was not a part of The Piece Good Shops, Inc. now located in North Carolina. An agreement had been written on May 31, 1961 with respect to the sale and purchase of the Charleston store in the event of his death. As I understood what little was told to me, Daddy owned and operated the Charleston store until his death. At this time, the Executors were to decide whether to keep the store, sell the store, or close the store. They closed the store by liquidating the business and the proceeds were divided among the remaining Executors. The Will was witnessed by Charles B. Stacy, David B. Shapiro and J. Hornor Davis, IV.

Dudley and John left the house shortly after the burial, but, before their leaving, Mother's bedroom was locked with a key. For what purpose, I do not know, except for the obvious. They wanted to be assured that no one would enter her room. In addition, Dudley approached Betty Lee and asked her to return a ring which Mother had allowed her to wear. For their fortieth birthdays, Mother had bought Dudley III and John each a ring set with a approximate one carat blue white diamond of exceptional quality. Dudley refused to wear such a large diamond, so he gave it to Mother with the promise the ring would be returned to him when he so desired or after Mother's demise. As I remember, Mother was fond of one of Betty's rings, so they traded until the proper time. It so happened that the manner and the chosen time in which the ring was claimed by Dudley, greatly disturbed my sister. On occasions, such as this one, actions often occur without deep or conscious consideration. I want to believe that this is why Dudley behaved as he did.

The reading of the Wills took place after Daddy's death. I was not aware of when or where it happened. I received copies of the Wills. Dudley III, John, and Betty divided the personal belongings. Later my sister shared with me some of the items she had inherited. There was a diamond and platinum ring which Mother called her cocktail ring. After joining AA, it became her dinner ring. It is a lovely ring and I enjoy wearing it for its beauty and its belonging to Mother. Another gift from Betty Lee was a twenty dollar gold piece set in a gold bezel hanging from a gold chain. It was the gold coin Mother was wearing when she visited me in the hospital after Thanksgiving 1982. Mother had instructed Betty to give it to me, if she did not survive the last operation. I couldn't begin to list what I received through her. There was Daddy's felt hat which I in turn mailed to Dudley's grandson Dudley V. Betty was extremely generous. She also inherited the task of preparing the house for sale. As she was working in the real estate business at the time, she knew what enticed potential buyers.

For several days Tia and I assisted Betty in cleaning out the attic and dispersing other articles that no one seemed to desire or had room to store. During the last days, she arrived with a paper for me to sign, given to her by Dudley and John. It was a release saying (in essence) I would make no further claims on the estates. My heart felt as if it had been pierced. There may have been rumors of my considering such an action, but it was only what others outside the family believed logical. I refused to sign the release.

Returning to Huntington, I called Noel Copen, as Michael Perry had left the law firm by this time, to become a banker. I explained to him the situation in which I was involved. I was in the midst of preparing to defend my dissertation and needed no further distractions. I asked Mr. Copen to correspond with my brothers, explaining the situation and that, if they wanted, I would return the mink coat. As far as I am concerned, nothing else has been said about the release.

The residence itself was given to John Simms with instructions. (I know not why Betty Lee did not receive the house as Daddy died after Mother, and in his Will, it was left to Betty. Perhaps, it had something to do with the thirty-day clause in Mother's Will. Or, perhaps, I was given an earlier will of Daddy's, without changes. Anyway, Betty Lee was an Executor, so she must have been aware of the situation.) The instructions were, if Betty wanted, she was to live in the house free of rent, but all expenses would become her responsibility. She said to me, "Patty, as much as I would enjoy living here, I do not have enough income to maintain this house. Therefore, John will sell the house, invest the money he receives, and I will be given the interest until I die or remarry." When Betty died in January of 1991, the money received from the sale of the house was divided among Tracy (Betty's daughter), Dudley's children and John's children. My five children and Betty's two sons were denied the privilege of sharing in their grandparents' estate. The amount of money divided among the seven grandchildren was not great in size, but the lack of "Mercy, Pity, Peace and Love" has had greater power than the gift of money could ever have created. (Note the stanzas of poetry by W. Blake presented at the beginning of each part of this book and at the end.)

13

Concluding

There is one more letter which is pertinent to the writing of this book. Though it evokes emotions I have attempted to dispel, I have decided to proceed with its inclusion. In February of 1976, I took a six-week leave of absence from teaching to have a hysterectomy. I was in Cabell Huntington Hospital for about a week, after which I returned home to recuperate. When I felt well enough, I planned to fly to Tampa, Florida to complete my recovery before having to returning to my position at Huntington High School. Linda and Karry, who were living there at this time, had invited me to visit them. Mother was staying at the condo on Pompano Beach, which was owned by my parents and my brothers. When Mother heard of my coming to Tampa, she called saying, "I just heard today that you are going to stay with Li .da and Karry. Why don't you fly to Pompano for a few days and stay with me here in the condo? It would be wonderful for us to be together again." Once more my heart was filled with hope and expectation, but the dream became another disappointment. Just before I left Huntington to go to Tampa, I received this letter from Dudley. I can't begin to describe the dejection, the hurt, the sorrow, the pain, including the embarrassment, I felt as I read the letter he had written to me.

March 5, 1976

Mrs. Keith G. Harrison
1016 West 3rd Street
Huntington, W.Va.

Dear Patty,

This letter is concerning the invitation extended to you by Mother to visit our Florida condominium.

I know that under the circumstances you will agree that it is best how things worked out.

Patty, we do love you and have forgiven you and Keith for past events. Perhaps we can discuss this sometime. I would appreciate your honesty in advising me if there is any reason why I should not visit you when in Huntington.

I hope that this letter finds you and you family doing well.

Love,

Dudley L. Simms, III

Even today, twenty-six years later, the emotions return. My first impulse is to question his reasoning, but I know that is futile. I remember talking to Mother; though she was as unhappy as I was (or she seemed to be), she offered no solution. She had accepted his decision, as did I.

My trip to visit Linda's and Karry's home in Tampa did reach realization. They both worked, so I was free to rest and read all day, every day. When they returned home, we visited and enjoyed being together. The warmth of the sun was healing to my body, and God lifted my soul.

If I say Dudley was wrong, I am judging and I do not believe God wants us to judge one and another. Jesus says in Matthew 7:1-2, "Do not judge or you too will be judged. For in the same way you judge others, you will be judged, and with the measure you use, it will be measured to you." God sent his son to show us how to live, to show us the way. Thus, I ask again, "What does God call me to do? What is his purpose for his children? The answer is loud and clear in Ephesians 1, verse 10. "Bring all things in heaven and on earth together under one head, even Christ." How do I help accomplish this? I know he would not approve of my condemning my earthly family for we are told to live a life worthy of being God's child. We must love each other as Christ loves us, regardless of mistakes, actions or words (Ephesians 5:1, 4:32, 5:21). We are to be imitators of God; therefore, as dearly loved children, we are to live a life of love, just as Christ loves us.

Certainly, each time I read Dudley's letter, I see his words: "We do love you and have forgiven you and Keith for past events." However, I continue to feel the pain of his actions and find it difficult to understand his decision. Was he not punishing me for what he judged me as doing? And, what have I done? I do not know. I constantly attempt to do what I believe Christ chooses me to do. I trust in the Lord. I strive to put God first in my heart and that means I also strive to visualize God in all things and in all people and pray for faith. Being his child, I know my prayers shall be answered. Now, if I can only remember to have patience and allow God to do what he wants, when he wants and how he wants. After all, he is my Lord and the Father who desires only the best for me and mine.

In January of 2001, I received a phone call from Dudley. He began the conversation as if we had never been apart, but finally he confessed his true reason for phoning. With tears in his voice, he said, "The doctors have told me I have cancer and believe I have about six weeks remaining here on earth." My first reaction was denial; I could not accept the prognosis as being correct. However, I immediately asked, "What can I do? What would you like for me to do?" He quickly responded, "I want to see you, but not until I look and feel better. I want people to remember me as I appeared before I became ill." He continued, "The doctors are not definite, but the cancer may have started in the bone; so, if you wouldn't mind, I would appreciate your sending a sample of your blood to determine if your blood type matches mine. Of course, I am very fortunate to have John as an identical twin, but the clinic also wants an analysis of your blood."

I was so happy he had called me and had considered me a possible donor; however, after the examinations and tests were completed, the doctors discovered they were unable to determine the origin of the cancer. I did send samples of my blood, but they were not needed.

During this same conversation in January, Dudley also approached the possibility of his dying. He asked, "When I die, will you come to my funeral? I want you to promise to be there." I responded, "Of course, I shall. I love you now, and I always will." At the time, I refused to believe his death was so close. How could he die before me? I was ten years older than he, so I should go to Heaven first.

Later, during the spring, I called Dudley several times, but seldom was I able to talk to him personally. I also sent letters, cards and notes. In addition, I contacted Troy (Barbara and Dudley's oldest child). In essence, the phone visits with her were the most informative. What I really wanted to do was visit him, but as often as I attempted, I never received the approval (which I felt was necessary).

Finally, Dudley called me on Saturday, June 23. As I picked up the receiver and heard his voice, so full of strength and joy, my heart jumped with love. He exclaimed (quickly, as usual), "Patty, this is Dudley. Barbara and I are coming to Charleston, and we want you, Keith and your family to meet us for lunch at Humphrey's Restaurant. You are to be our guests."

Describing the excitement I received as I listened to those words is impossible, at least for me; I thought the day of understanding had finally arrived. We would once again be united as brother and sister. Of course, being the eternal optimist I have always been, I believed we would only speak about loving, caring, sorrow, appreciation, future activities, but that was not what happened.

Before leaving for Charleston, I asked Keith if he wanted to go; he did not. Then I questioned, "Do you mind if I go? Would you think I would be disloyal?" He replied, "No. I understand why you want and need to go, and I hope you will understand why I do not." Of course, I understood; but, at the same time, I felt apprehensive to leave without him. I have always known life is better with Keith at my side. Still, I thought, this may be the last time I will see my brother alive. It is now or never. Also, if I do not go (I questioned), would I be refusing because I am attempting to punish Dudley as he has punished me? I am the one who repeatedly says God does not want us to judge each other. If we are to bring Heaven and earth together, we are to love each other regardless of our faults or mistakes. There is no other way. As for Keith's decision, I personally believe he showed great wisdom, once again.

Dudley explained that he had not phoned us earlier because he wanted to be certain he would feel well and would appear somewhat as he had in previous days. At this time, he was under treatment at The Anderson Cancer Center in Houston, Texas and was encouraged by the results. He himself drove the car from Winston-Salem to Charleston and even drove part of the return trip on the same day.

Those of our family who accompanied me to lunch were Tia, her husband Joe Daulton, and one of their twin daughters Laura; also Karry (our oldest son) and his wife Linda joined us. Scott remained at home with Keith. As Sean, his wife Laura and their children were returning from Long Beach, North Carolina, and Dirk and his family were living in Kure Beach, North Carolina, they were not available to decline or accept the invitation. All of Betty Lee's children were invited and did attend. (Betty had died in 1991.) There were John Sears, Brent Sears, Tracy Sears-Self, her husband Glenn and all of Betty's grandchildren. In addition, looking beautiful and filled with energy (as usual), was Aunt Jackie, Mother's younger sister who lives in Charleston. It was an outstanding group of people and a memorable afternoon; however, Dudley was not there to mend the breaks between my family and his. And, by the end of the lunch, everyone there realized it.

As we entered the door, Dudley and Barbara came forth with hugs, kisses and welcoming remarks. Dudley did ask, "Wasn't Keith able to come?" and I responded, "No, he has not been well for several months; he has a double hernia, and Scott decided to remain at home with him. I am so sorry, but perhaps the next time. However, he is happy you are feeling better and prays your recovery continues." Dudley then replied "Tell him that Barbara and I asked about him."

Barbara and Dudley appeared tan, excited, and positive. It was truly a gift from the Lord to see and be with them once again. Dudley constantly praised the healing power of God, which had allowed him to recuperate after his last treatment of chemo and radiation. We also chatted about events in the past and the present, but there was no mention of the suits or the wills. His purpose for visiting us was to give witness and thanks for God's blessings, which included his health, wealth and family.

After the visit in June, I called and wrote but received no response, nor approval to visit Dudley. Perhaps I should not have allowed this to stop me, but I chose not to chance another rejection. It appeared that this was how Dudley wanted it to end. I wonder what Jesus would have done and what he shall say to me when I meet him. Will my Lord be disappointed in my decision?

Dudley died in April of 2002, almost a month before his sixty-fifth birthday. Keith and I did attend the service. We were joined by Tia (our daughter), her husband Joe, Karry (our first son), his wife Linda, their daughter Ashleigh, her husband Travis Menke (and even their baby son), Karry's youngest son Chase, and our second son Scott. Dirk and his sons Chanse and Clark drove from Kure Beach, North Carolina and met us at the church. I had invited each of our children and their families, but the final decision was theirs. Sean and his family had previous engagements that could not be canceled; this was understandable. I personally did not believe Dudley would miss them; the ties between Dudley and our children were not strong. However, the support of those who were able to be with me at this time was greatly appreciated for God's presence was felt moving among us. Keith and I both agree God has blessed us with the gift of a loving and caring family.

I must attempt to describe the funeral and the service. It was held at the Calvary Baptist Church in Winston on Sunday, April 7 at one o'clock. We sat directly behind the immediate family who occupied the first three pews. I truly enjoyed watching the children, spouses and grandchildren of Dudley, Barbara, John and Victoria. Each and every one was so beautiful; but, what drew my attention the most was the evidence of the Simms gene in the sprinkling of golden red hair on the heads of the children. God's way is magnificent and apparent.

As for the service, it was Southern Baptist in every detail. There were sixty-five members in the choir and a full orchestra. Two ministers spoke, as well as our brother John. It was a celebration of Dudley's life and God's love. I imagine Dudley was in heaven, smiling from ear to ear.

After the funeral, Dudley's and John's families entered the limousines and left for the farm. All those who attended the service were invited to the burial which took place at a private cemetery located on the farm. (Barbara and Dudley's oldest grandson was buried there when he died in September of 1994.) Neither I nor my family went to Dudley's burial or to the buffet afterwards. Once again, I told our children and their families the decision was theirs. However, as I was not certain of how my appearance would affect others, I chose not to attend. The purpose of the occasion was to remember Dudley's life, not the affair which had divided the family. Also, I feared I might not have been welcomed. I had not been informed personally of Dudley's death. In fact, one of my friends called to be certain I knew. The only member of Dudley's family to contact me was Dudley and Barbara's son, Dudley IV. He called me on a cell phone from his van on the evening of the visitation, just as we arrived in Winston-Salem. His voice reminded me so much of Dudley; I could almost believe Dudley was calling me. However, instead of Patty, I heard, "Aunt Patty, we are glad you and the family were able to be here. We hope to see you tonight at the visitation. How are your rooms?" After assuring him of our comfort, I expressed our sorrow and explained, "As we have just arrived and are exhausted from the drive, we will not see you tonight, but we will see you tomorrow." Yet, there was another reason for our not attending the visitation. I have never wholeheartedly accepted that part of the funeral services. We, as Christians, believe, after our physical death, our spiritual and eternal life begins with our Lord in Heaven. What believers could possibly mourn such an exchange? If the visitation is a social affair, as some are, the gathering after the funeral serves this purpose. Of course, I feel compassion for those who remain on earth, but I had expressed this feeling to the family by other means and could easily imagine how emotionally drained the family would be during an evening of "visiting." I had promised Dudley I would be at the funeral, and so Keith and I were there with love and praise and accompanied by many members of our family.

Before and after the funeral, I had expected to talk with the family at the church, but this expectation became an impossibility. The families did not arrive early to the church and were not available before the service; they were driven from the farm in limousines, entered during the prelude, marched out of the church during the postlude, and then returned to the farm. Troy was the only one to actually acknowledge our presence; her recognition and smile were gratefully appreciated by all of us.

After the service, Keith and I and our family met at a restaurant for a early supper before our driving back to Huntington. Dirk and his sons returned to Kure Beach. Linda and Karry had driven from Huntington to Blacksburg on the previous day as they had scheduled a meeting for Chase (their youngest child) at VPI, where he will be a freshman this coming fall. On Sunday, they drove to Winston-Salem, attended the service, and after supper, returned to Huntington. All of us passed each other on the road. Ashleigh, her husband Travis and their baby son Travee had to travel all the way back to Columbus, Ohio. I was proud that so many members of our family took the time out of their busy lives to remember my brother Dudley. In my opinion, it was worth every minute of their sacrifices to see this branch of the family for at least one time. I understand that one of our grandsons asked his father, "Who are all these people anyway?" Perhaps, it is best for me not to know how this question was answered or if it were answered. After all, a complete response would require months, if not years. Perhaps Dudley's obituary would have sufficed; however, some of the information offered was questionable and misleading. Let us just say, "It ended and all arrived home safely, but tired."

My story is drawing to its end, at least for now. Many people (some I have never met) have asked why I did not contest Mother and Daddy's Wills. Mentally, my first response is: "I did not want to do it." As the estates belonged to my parents, they had the right to decide what to do with what they had earned. My brothers did greatly influence the writing of the wills, but it is evident they had much to do with the growth of the company. Their goal was to gain a monetary fortune, or at least this is what one may assume as the PGS Incorporated was sold and is now removed from the history of family businesses. My brothers do have another enterprise, but it is not concerned with the merchandising of yard goods and notions.

When my father became extremely ill and was no longer able to work in the Charleston store, my mother was asked to attend a meeting of the company in Winston-Salem. My brothers were anxious to secure their futures, and they realized my mother wanted to preserve her life style and my father's as long as one or both lived. Thus, Mother was offered an agreement, which she signed on each and every page. I know Mother felt she would outlive Daddy, so the Charleston store would be consumed by the Jordan company, as this was the agreement at that time. Even the executors of the Wills were chosen by my brothers; Mother continually asked, "Who is Bob Bias, the young man selected as an executor of my will?" and I would respond, "A very close friend of

Dudley's." Sometimes she would ask "What is the name of the young man whom Dudley selected to be an executor?" And I would answer.

As for me, my inheritance was the rich relationship my sister Betty Lee and I received by being privileged to enjoy the attention and companionship of my parents during the period when their lives were not so complicated or not so occupied with civic organizations, mergers and illnesses. Certainly, Keith and I and our children have received many material gifts from Mother and Daddy since the beginning of our marriage in 1946 which have assisted in our enjoyment of life. I was not disappointed in what I received, but I was hurt by their words which were directed to me.

Another reason I did not contest the Wills was I had this idea that when Dudley III and John had received their inheritances, the discord between us would end. I had basically thought they were angry because the Circuit Court of Cabell County had decided in Keith's favor; so, with the material wealth given to them in the Wills, they received much more than what they had been forced to pay Keith. The stress did decrease, but the relationship between us has remained distant. I am sorry to say I know not why.

In addition, I confess to being suspicious of large amounts of material wealth. It seems to me that only a few (if any) are able to find true fulfillment in an environment of money and things. I attempt to focus on inner wealth, the spirit of my Savior living within me. This does not signify my never yearning for articles or activities which money attains, because at intervals I have had these desires; but, at the same time, I realize that such riches do not insure an eternal life filled with my Lord's blessings.

Often I pray that I have not deprived our children and their children of what they desire and perhaps deserve, but I truly believe that God knows best what we need and do not need. He wants all of his children to share in his blessings, and all of us shall be his heirs if we turn to him and proclaim our belief, our love, our obedience, our surrender to Our Lord. There can be no greater life or no greater future than that of a life without an end in eternity with God our Father.

The Divine Image
By
William Blake

To Mercy, Pity, Peace, and Love
All pray in their distress;
And to these virtues of delight
Return their thankfulness.
For Mercy, Pity, Peace, and Love
Is God, our father dear.
And Mercy, Pity, Peace, and Love
Is Man, his child and care.
For Mercy has a human heart,
Pity a human face,
And Love, the human form divine,
And Peace, the human dress.
Then every man of every clime,
That prays in his distress
Prays to the human form divine,
Love, Mercy, Pity, Peace.
All must love the human form,
In heathen, Turk, or Jew;
Where Mercy, Love and Pity dwell
There God is dwelling too.

—1789

Information And Inspiration

Abrams, M. H., General Editor. *The Norton Anthology of English Literature*. New York: W.W. Norton and company, Inc., 1962.

Alexander, Geraldine D. (Notary Public). *Last Will and Testament of Dudley L. Simms*. Charleston, Kanawha County, West Virginia, June 14, 1978.

"All Charges being Denied by Simmses." *The Charleston Gazette*, Charleston, West Virginia, Tuesday Morning, Nov. 4, 1975, pgs. A1, A2.

Bailey and Thomas Attorneys. The Last Will and Testament of Opal Marie Simms. Witnesses by David Wesley Bailey, Jr. of Winston-Salem, North Carolina, Wesley L. Bailey of Winston-Salem, North Carolina, et. al., April 17, 1982.

Bonhoeffer, Dietrich. *Life Together*. San Francisco: Harper Collins Publisher, 1954.

Brother Lawrence, Teresa of Avila. *The Practice of the Presence of God and The Way of Perfection*. Nashville: Thomas Nelson Publishers, 1999.

"Ex-Huntington Man Admits Taking $40,000." *Charleston Gazette*, Charleston, West Virginia, 1974

Fox, Emmet. *Stake Your Claim*. New York: First HarperCollins Paperback Edition, 1992.

Haught, James A. "Dudley Simms, Sons Sued." *Charleston Gazette*. Charleston, West Virginia, Saturday, Nov. 1, 1975, pgs. A1, A2.

Huddleston, Bolen, Beatty, Porter & Copen. *Agreement Between Keith G. Harrison and Huddleston, Bolen, Beatty, Porter & Copen*. Huntington, West Virginia: February 11, 1971

Huddeston; Jackson N. *Letter Re. Dudley L. Simms, et. al, v. Harrison*(Mailed to Wilham c. Payne et. al.), May 26, 1971.

Mantius, Pete. "N.Y. Firm Buys Piece Goods Shops." *Winston-Salem Journal*. Winston-Salem, North Carolina: Tuesday, August 24, 1982, p. 15.

Matthews, Glen K. (Notary Public). *The Deposition of Dudley L.Simms, In the Circuit Court of Cabell County, West Virginia*, Civil Action #25007, March 10, 1971.

Matthews, Glen K. (Notary Public). *The Deposition of Keith G. Harrison, In the Curcuit Court of Cabell County, West Virginia*, Civil Action #25007, March 10, 1971.

Nuzum, Bob. "Dudley's Rule Is Golden." *The New Charleston*, Volume 35, Number 4, July-August 1972, pp. 26-29.

O'Brien, John. *At Home in the Heart of Appalachia*. New York; Alfred A. Knoff (a division of Random House, Inc.), 2001.

Payne, Wilham C. *Letter Re. Dudley L. Simms, et. al. v. Harrison*, (Mailed to Jackson N. Huddleston et. al.), May 28, 1971.

"Public Notice." *The Herald Dispatch*, Huntington, West Virginia, Friday Nov. 7, 1975.

Raine, Kathleen. *William Blake*. New York: Praeger Publishers, 1971.

The Student Bible. Grand Rapids, Michigan, Zondervan Bible Publishers, 1989.

"$10 Million Claim Filed." *Charleston Gazette*, Charleston, West Virginia, 1975

Biography

Patricia Simms Harrison was born in Charleston, West Virginia and received her early education in the local schools, graduating from Stonewall Jackson High School 1945. She attended Ward-Belmont in Nashville, Morris-Harvey in Charleston and received a bachelor's degree from Marshall University in 1964. She later earned a master's degree from Marshall and continued her studies at the University of Kentucky in foreign language education. She has studied abroad at the University of Madrid in conjunction with New York University and received a doctorate in 1983 from Marshall University and West Virginia University. She has taught in the fields of Spanish, English and history at public schools in Cabell County, West Virginia and in Beaufort County, South Carolina. She has also instructed several classes in education at Marshall University and in Spanish for the University of South Carolina, Beaufort campus.

0-595-26275-9